Dr Goh Keng Swee, founder of IEAP, IEAPE and EAI

Prof Zheng Yongnian (left) with Singapore's Prime Minister Lee Hsien Loong at the FutureChina Global Forum organised by Business China on 10 July 2012 at Shangri-La Hotel Singapore.

Dr Goh Keng Swee, founder of IEAP, IEAPE and EAI

Published by

World Scientific Publishing Co. Pte. Ltd.
5 Toh Tuck Link, Singapore 596224
USA office: 27 Warren Street, Suite 401-402, Hackensack, NJ 07601
UK office: 57 Shelton Street, Covent Garden, London WC2H 9HE

British Library Cataloguing-in-Publication Data
A catalogue record for this book is available from the British Library.

THE EAST ASIAN INSTITUTE
A Goh Keng Swee Legacy

ISBN 978-981-4725-71-2
ISBN 978-981-4740-68-5 (pbk)

In-house Editor: Dong Lixi

Typeset by Stallion Press
Email: enquiries@stallionpress.com

The East Asian Institute
A Goh Keng Swee Legacy

East Asian Institute
National University of Singapore, Singapore

World Scientific

NEW JERSEY · LONDON · SINGAPORE · BEIJING · SHANGHAI · HONG KONG · TAIPEI · CHENNAI · TOKYO

The East Asian Institute
A Goh Keng Swee Legacy

(From left) Prof Wang Gungwu, Minister Mentor Lee Kuan Yew and Prof John Wong at the East Asian Institute's 10th Anniversary Lectures

(From left) Prof John Wong, Prof Zheng Yongnian and Mr Lye Liang Fook with Minister Mentor Lee Kuan Yew (seated) at the 15th Anniversary Celebration of the Establishment of the Suzhou Industrial Park on 26 May 2009 in Suzhou

Dr Goh Keng Swee in a discussion with scholars

Contents

Preface   xi

The Making of the East Asian Institute   1
Lim Tai Wei

Goh Keng Swee and Contemporary China Studies
in Singapore   33
John Wong

Singapore's Road to "China Watching"   69
John Wong

Preface

The birth pangs of a book publication begin with its creators and the rationale for its existence. In the case of this writing, the parents that give birth to the concept and idea for a book on the institutional history of East Asian Institute (EAI) are the first and second generation guardians of EAI, Professors Wang Gungwu, John Wong and Zheng Yongnian. Under their guardianship, the institute has grown to become a full epistemological plant of knowledge on contemporary China.

This book is about the process of the careful nurturing of a depository of knowledge on East Asia through the inspiring and educator role of Professor Wang Gungwu as EAI's first director as well as the meticulous administrative hands of Professor John Wong. Wang's iconic scholarship and his depth of intellectual experience as former vice chancellor of Hong Kong University (1986 to 1995) undergirded EAI's ability to attract institutional and individual scholars to the institute to conduct world-class research and provide significant insight into the emergence of the Chinese market economy. Wong's deep Sinology background and economist training oriented the research output towards policy relevance.

Zheng has inherited the hands of the nurturer as the director, while Wang assumes overall chairmanship and Wong remains as the institute's professorial fellow. This transition marks the second phase of the institutional growth of EAI — a collaborative and collective effort of the founder, executor and inheritor of EAI's depository of knowledge and scholarship.

The hard work behind the nurturing of this institute that eventually grew to become one of the top five think tanks in the world is sometimes invisible, unwritten and under-appreciated but the contributions and results are clear and relevant to the scholarly world. The works of EAI's originating guardians as well as the future endeavours of its current directorship thus need to be chronicled for future generations of scholars to learn from this intellectual experience of managing an institution as complex as EAI.

The detailed historiography of EAI in this publication represents the multiple histories of EAI, China's developmental path since the initiation of market reforms as well as Singapore's collaborative interface with China's development.

The Making of the East Asian Institute

Lim Tai Wei

Adjunct Research Fellow, East Asian Institute, Singapore

Summary

This paper is an institutional study of the East Asian Institute (EAI), National University of Singapore (NUS). It examines both physical facilities such as the library as well as the profiles of its founding academic members. The uniqueness of the institute is also analysed in this chapter. EAI as an institution interacts with visiting Chinese scholars, through regular staff members who have multiple identities as western-trained Chinese scholars, and are culturally familiar with Singapore's intellectual and policy-making environment.

Professors Wang Gungwu and John Wong, the institute's first and second generation pioneers, anchored the developmental phase of EAI. The institute was nurtured by Wang, a senior scholar who used to helm a major university institution in Hong Kong and Wong, an experienced economist with a passion for Sinology and an efficient administrator trained personally by Dr Goh Keng Swee, one of the founding fathers of independent Singapore.

The results of this unique marriage of senior scholars, institutional support and Singapore's unique position are research monographs with specialised information on China that is relevant to Singapore's policy-making community, background briefs for the government ministries and journal papers for the academic communities. The wealth of information and ideas reflect the views of senior Chinese scholars and are accurately and precisely presented in a neutral format in the English language.

When the capacity-building capabilities reached maturity, the second generation of scholars took over the executive leadership led by Professor Zheng Yongnian. Zheng encompasses the values laid down in the first generation as a mainland native-born Chinese scholar familiar with Chinese cultural nuances. Educated in Princeton University and residing in Singapore, Zheng is also familiar with Western academic traditions and exposed to the city-state's intellectual and policy-making pulses.

The combination of a senior historian, veteran economist and political scientist with nuanced insights has become the "software" accounting for EAI's success through the developmental stage to maturity. This article argues that it is this stakeholder interest in a unique neutral intermediating platform that cross-pollinates ideas from the West, China, East Asia and Singapore and into EAI's third stage of evolution.

Institutional Setup

A brief backgrounder.[1] The East Asian Institute (EAI) was set up in April 1997 as an autonomous research organisation under a statute of the National University of Singapore. It is the successor of the former Institute of East Asian Political Economy (IEAPE), which was itself the successor of the Institute of East Asian Philosophies (IEAP), originally established by Dr Goh Keng Swee in 1983 for the study of Confucianism. The main mission of EAI is to promote academic and policy-oriented research on contemporary China and other East Asian economies. More specifically, EAI scholars conduct studies on various aspects of political, economic and social changes in China arising from its economic reform and open-door policy, the regional and global implications of the economic rise of China, and the cultural and commercial networks of ethnic Chinese from a global perspective. The institute also monitors developments in Hong Kong, Taiwan and Macau, and China's relations with Japan, Korea and ASEAN. To promote academic exchange and to enable its research findings to reach out to a wider segment of the public, EAI organises seminars and publishes research papers on a regular basis. EAI also participates in joint research projects with government ministries and statutory boards in Singapore, promotes collaborative programmes with similar institutions in the region as well as organises regional and international conferences and workshops on East Asian issues. The long-term vision of

---

[1] The brief backgrounder is extracted from the corporate booklet of East Asian Institute, Singapore, East Asian Institute (Singapore: EAI, 2010), p. 3.

EAI is to develop into the region's foremost research institute on East Asian development.

Rooting in the region and extending to regional networks. As a think tank, EAI is a unique institution based in Singapore with deep roots in contemporary China research that are effectively transnational, reaching out to the scholarly and policy-making communities in Northeast Asia as well as the global pool of individuals working on contemporary China and East Asian issues. An important aspect of the institute's formation is the presence of an international pool of academicians exchanging ideas in this institution, including short-term visiting scholars. The composition of EAI scholars is thus not only from China, but also Singapore and other parts of the world. The institution's formation itself is historical and ground-breaking as the second full-time government advisory think tank after the Institute of Southeast Asian Studies (ISEAS). The diversity, quality and quantity of its *background briefs*, reports on issues of topical interest pertaining to China and East Asia, written for government agencies in this respect is one of the successful features of this advisory role. It is indicative of EAI's strong link with the government from the beginning, a feature unlike no other research institutes in Singapore. While providing advisory services to the state, EAI stands in a unique position and enjoys non-state affiliated autonomy, dispensing advice from a non-governmental organisational platform.

In that way, it embodies the objectivity and neutrality of a scholarly organisation, while serving the state's needs for practical knowledge and information about China when it was still engrossed with domestic political developments. In the same way, it was also a depository of knowledge about other northeast Asian developments. Academic and professional objectivity and neutrality preserves EAI's standing amongst academicians and tertiary institutions while the acquisition of practical knowledge keeps the research relevant to the Singapore government by grounding the briefs and the writings in practitioners' experience and developing a strong tradition in policy research.

Aside from the policy advisory role to the Singapore government, the regionalisation of EAI's role and functions are also visible in its participation in regional networks of think tanks, including the Network of East Asian Think-Tanks (NEAT) which carries out policy recommendations to ASEAN (Association of Southeast Asian Nations), China, Japan and Korea, and cooperation with Konrad-Adenauer-Stiftung (of Germany), the European Policy Centre (of Brussels) and the European Union Centre (of Singapore).[2] This introductory chapter surveys the milestones achieved by EAI over the years but does not pretend to be comprehensive in listing out the remarkable achievements that this unique institution has attained. It is also cognisant of the achievements that EAI has accumulated over the years under three generations of leading figures in its management.

Milestones

On the 15th anniversary of EAI, Professor Tan Chorh Chuan (president of the National University of Singapore) noted the two broad directions of the institute in

---

[2] East Asian Institute (EAI), *Redefining Traditions Embracing Modernity Commemorating EAI's 15th Anniversary* (Singapore: East Asian Institute National University of Singapore, 2012), p. 7.

"undertaking rigorous academic and policy-oriented research on developments with a strong focus on contemporary China" and "fostering lively intellectual debate and discussion among researchers, influential leaders and stakeholders, through its many dialogue sessions, seminars and conferences".[3] The twin goals of academic output and hosting policy exchanges were gradually built up over the years though the capabilities were achieved quite early in its founding phase. By the fifth anniversary of the EAI as an autonomous institution within the National University of Singapore, the output achieved by EAI was considerable with 25 academic books, 126 EAI working papers and 32 EAI occasional papers which were circulated to the Singaporean government circles (including cabinet ministers, ministers of state and ranking civil servants), 127 informative and policy-oriented *EAI Background Briefs* and 280 weekly public seminars.[4] In the words of former Minister of Trade and Industry in Singapore George Yeo:

> I look forward to reading EAI's latest Briefs on China. Many
> provide interesting information about the latest developments

---

[3] Tan Chorh Chuan, *Redefining Traditions Embracing Modernity Commemorating EAI's 15th Anniversary* (Singapore: East Asian Institute National University of Singapore, 2012), p. 3.
[4] Hsuan Owyang, "Speech by Mr Hsuan Owyang, Chairman, EAI Management Board EAI's 5th Anniversary Lectures 17 July 2002, Mandarin Hotel Your Excellencies", National University of Singapore East Asian Institute website, p. 1, available at http://www.eai.nus.edu.sg/Hsuan%20 Owyang.pdf, accessed 13 October 2014. Comparatively, EAI's predecessors, IEAP and IEAPE published a total of 15 internal study papers, 21 commentaries, 107 *background briefs*, eight China news analysis and 15 discussion papers. In the EAI library, a physical count revealed that there were 17 IEAP/IEAPE books on display (six were written in Chinese).

there. Some contain insights which are important for the formulation of MTI policies. EAI researchers brief MTI staff regularly.[5]

By 2012, this output had increased to an average of two *Background Briefs* per week.[6] With the collective efforts of its scholars under the leadership of its management, the institute has produced a total of 1,011 *background briefs*, the number reached at this point of writing. On the academic front, EAI's own academic journal, *China: an international journal*, published since 2003 has been indexed in the Social Sciences Citation Index.[7] Since its inception, EAI has provided both academic/theoretical as well as practical/policy researches. Consequently, it has a unique position that straddles both practitioners' as well as scholarly viewpoints. Perhaps, one of its major platforms for promoting Singapore-China relations is through the organisation of the Singapore-China Forum with its counterparts in China to discuss ideas and debates over views alongside officials from both countries.[8]

EAI's Principal Drivers

The founding of EAI was shaped by Singapore's historical context in many ways. Both Professor Wang Gungwu and

[5] John Wong, Aw Beng Teck and Lai Hongyi (eds), *Analysing China Commemorating EAI's 5th Anniversary* (Singapore: East Asian Institute, 2002), p. 3.
[6] East Asian Institute (EAI), *Redefining Traditions Embracing Modernity Commemorating EAI's 15th Anniversary*, p. 6.
[7] East Asian Institute (EAI), *Redefining Traditions Embracing Modernity Commemorating EAI's 15th Anniversary*, p. 6.
[8] East Asian Institute (EAI), *Redefining Traditions Embracing Modernity Commemorating EAI's 15th Anniversary*, p. 7.

Professor John Wong experienced societal pulses and changes in Singapore's society, from the developmental phase, to Confucianism promotion and to practical engagement with China. Using this paradigm, the research work at this institute was useful for analysing and understanding the rise of China and the external impact of China's immediate environment. At the recent EAI annual conference, Wang was described as a scholar who experienced a number of significant 20th century events that included the Pacific War, Malaya's and Singapore's independence in the age of decolonisation, Cold War and the rise of China. He brought the participant standpoint view and a historical context to EAI. In the same conference, Wong was described as a prolific researcher with a significant research output and a veteran Sinologist or China watcher (Wong is careful with the term 'China watching' as he views the term as having negative nuances in the post-Cold War context. This is mentioned in his chapter in this volume).

Goh Keng Swee. Dr Goh Keng Swee, a former deputy prime minister of Singapore, has often been referred to as the "economic architect" of the island-state.[9] The historical origins of EAI is intertwined with Goh's role in its founding phase. The authoritative National Library Board website listed Goh as the chairman of the board of governors, IEAP (later renamed IEAPE) from 1983 to 1992; executive chairman and chairman of board of governors, IEAPE and chairman of East Asian Consultancy

---

[9] Jenny Tien and Valerie Chew, "Goh Keng Swee", National Library Singapore website, available at http://eresources.nlb.gov.sg/infopedia/articles/SIP_662_2005-01-11.html, accessed 13 October 2014.

(S) Pte Ltd from 1992 to 1995; and deputy chairman of IEAPE from 1996 to 1997.[10] According to Tan Siok Sun's important biographical volume on Goh, after Goh retired from active politics and public service, he focused his attention on IEAP established in July 1983 to research on "Confucian ethics and Asian values".[11] In 1992, this institute was reconfigured to look at contemporary China in the renamed IEAPE.[12] The 2010 informational booklet released by EAI stated that:

> The Institute of East Asian Philosophies (IEAP) was set up as a privately constituted non-profit resource and research centre for the study of Oriental philosophies with emphasis on the translation, interpretation and evaluation of Confucian ethics.[13]

The study of Confucian values was interpreted in various ways by scholarly and media sources. Vogel associated this venture with the idea of governance (discussed later in the section), and Wong's authoritative chapter in this book discussed the issue in relation to policies and contents introduced to the school curriculum as well as other public policy functions. With the reconfiguration of the

---

[10] National Library Board Singapore, "Goh Keng Swee", National Library Singapore website, available at http://eresources.nlb.gov.sg/infopedia/articles/SIP_662_2005-01-11.html, accessed 13 October 2014.
[11] For further reading: Tan Siok Sun, *Goh Keng Swee A Portrait* (Singapore: Editions Didier Millet, 2007), p. 166.
[12] Tan Siok Sun, *Goh Keng Swee A Portrait* (Singapore: Editions Didier Millet, 2007), p. 166.
[13] East Asian Institute, Singapore, East Asian Institute (Singapore: EAI), 2010, p. 4.

institute in 1992, directions were further clarified. Goh indicated them in his paper titled *Research Priorities*:

> We are now in a position to identify areas of research priorities. A small institute like the IEAPE with limited resources of finance and manpower must focus its attention on a few small areas. Ranging over the vast areas of the Chinese economy and political system would waste what little resources we have.[14]

Goh was a renaissance man: a politician, a scholar, a public intellectual, a promoter of values and an economic adviser to Chinese Vice Premier Gu Mu and his Office of Special Economic Zones in the State Council[15] between 1985 and 1990.[16] With his accumulated practitioner and policy knowledge on China, Goh was also an adviser to the Singapore's dealings with China and had regular Wednesday lunchtime dialogues with the then Senior Minister Lee Kuan Yew, founding father of modern Singapore.[17] Because of his important roles in many capacities, different sectors of society visualised his contributions in many ways. In this writing, only his contributions to EAI are discussed, while fully acknowledging the fact that other achievements are equally important.

---

[14] Zheng Yongnian and John Wong (eds), *Goh Keng Swee on China Selected Essays* (Singapore: World Scientific, 2013), p. 118. (In 2013, Zheng and Wong edited a substantial number of Goh-written important papers; readers may refer to this collection for detailed ideas on Goh's works.)

[15] John Wong, "Goh Keng Swee and Contemporary China Studies in Singapore", a chapter in this volume.

[16] Zheng Yongnian and John Wong (eds), *Goh Keng Swee on China Selected Essays* (Singapore: World Scientific, 2013), p. 1.

[17] John Wong, "Goh Keng Swee and Contemporary China Studies in Singapore", a chapter in this volume.

The history of EAI cannot be discussed in the absence of a tribute to Goh and the historical narrative cannot omit the IEAPE phase, the predecessor of EAI. IEAPE was an important project under Goh before the advent of Wang Gungwu's directorship of EAI. Goh not only established IEAPE, but also nurtured it constantly, growing it from a scholarly platform for philosophical and cultural studies to a policy-oriented research institution. He laid the guidelines and started the tradition of focusing on policy-oriented research, which is still EAI's forte today among all the Singapore-based think tanks. He received the funding and built up the financial foundation of the institute and for the institute. In terms of capacity-building, because of Goh, EAI has enjoyed close rapport with the government bureaucracy and received support from the state. Through Goh, IEAPE (and later EAI) established close relations with the Singapore government (including senior civil servants) and, since then, EAI has built up its traditions in policy-oriented research, not only in textbook form but also in reports and dialogues with practical applications for governmental organisations. Besides institutional seeding, the human talent software was also carefully grown during the IEAPE's formative years. Zheng Yongnian, the current director of EAI, was also a member of IEAPE. Therefore, IEAPE contributions are found in both tangible and intangible realms.

Goh's role in the setting up (and sometimes direct involvement) in IEAP/IEAPE and later in effecting the smooth transition from IEAPE to EAI speaks for itself here. The IEAPE, which started contemporary China research, evolved from almost a closed-door organisation at a time when both Singapore and the region were not conducive to open discussion of China-related topics. It started as an institution with rudimentary research resources (both in terms of primary and secondary data availability and library facilities) and lacked experienced and linguistically competent researchers; the credit to its transformation into a full-blown research outfit like EAI goes to Goh for his ability in overcoming adversities. Goh overcame the obstacles at the start-up phase of IEAPE, e.g. Singapore's political and social climate factors stacked against China-watching and Sinology studies during the Cold War period, the lack of academic resources from data (China's pre-reform and early reform information gap) and access to indigenous scholars who are well-versed with policy studies and political nuances and, at the same time, able to articulate them to a global and Singaporean policy-making audience.[18]

But the sheer importance of the rise of China partially assisted Goh in pushing through the vision of establishing a contemporary China Institute in a dynamic external environment. Goh's vision of China's eventual rise after Deng Xiaoping's Southern Tour (the *Nanxun*) in 1979 convinced many in Singapore of the importance of studying the unfurling event contextualised within that exceptional period. Therefore, Goh's determination coupled with the convergence of timely external events opened the path to a succeeding director, Wang Gungwu, who comes with strong academic credentials and an international academic standing and extensive academic experience. This is

---

[18] Readers interested in detailed accounts of this aspect are recommended to consult John Wong's important chapters in this publication for a first-hand account of some of the obstacles faced in the pioneering phase of the institute.

particularly useful when EAI enters the second phase in 1997 to become part of the National University of Singapore (NUS).

When Goh passed away in 2010 at the age of 91, Singapore's local media published their narratives of Goh's role in EAI and its predecessors. The Singapore Press Holdings noted that Goh served as the chairperson of the IEAP in 1983 and led the Singapore government's promotion of Confucianism (the details of this initiative can be read in Wong's insightful chapter in this volume).[19] The media also noted that Goh made an important contribution in information dissemination for the Singapore government and other stakeholders at a historical point of time when knowledge and information about China was still limited. Goh's leadership (of EAI and its predecessors) transitioned to Wang Gungwu when EAI was set up and this represented the first successful leadership transition in the history of the institute. Wong represented top management continuity in this transition serving the institute under the leaderships of both Goh and Wang.

Wang Gungwu. Professor Wang is well-known to the scholarly world as a China scholar (some also associate him with diasporic Chinese studies) who started his senior scholarly career as the director of the School of Pacific Studies at the Australian National University and then vice chancellor of the University of Hong Kong; he is credited by Hsuan Owyang as the reason why EAI has been able to

---

[19] AsiaOne, "Goh Keng Swee's major contributions", Asiaone News website, available at http://news.asiaone.com/News/AsiaOne+News/Singapore/Story/A1Story20100514-216195.html, accessed 13 October 2014.

attract Chinese scholars and academicians from overseas.[20]
In 1995, Goh suggested to Wong the idea of recruiting
Wang while Goh stayed on as vice chairperson to oversee
the leadership transition.[21] Zheng Yongnian and Phua
Kok Khoo's volume described Wang's return to Singapore
in 1996.

> [Wang] Left Hong Kong on 2 January to take up the posi-
> tion of Executive Chairman of the Institute of East Asian
> Political Economy (IEAPE), 1996–1997. After it became the
> East Asian institute (EAI), an autonomous research centre of
> the National University of Singapore, re-established links
> with equivalent research centres and institutes in China.
> Regular meetings with the heads of various institutions,
> mainly in Beijing.[22]

Wang is a major figure in navigating EAI through the
formative decades. Before EAI was established in 1997,
Wang was intimately involved in various positions of chairmanship and board members with its two predecessor institutions, the IEAP and the IEAPE.[23] In 1999, under
Wang's watch, EAI signed its first memorandum of understanding (MOU) with the Chinese Academy of Social

[20] Owyang Hsuan, "Speech by Mr Hsuan Owyang, Chairman, EAI
Management Board EAI's 5th Anniversary Lectures 17 July 2002, Mandarin
Hotel Your Excellencies", p. 3.
[21] John Wong, "Goh Keng Swee and Contemporary China Studies in
Singapore", a chapter in this volume.
[22] Zheng Yongnian and Phua Kok Khoo (eds), *Wang Gungwu Educator and
Scholar* (Singapore: World Scientific, 2013. This is a part of a chronology of
Wang Gungwu on p. 359.
[23] East Asian Institute (EAI), *Redefining Traditions Embracing Modernity
Commemorating EAI's 15th Anniversary*, p. 4.

Sciences in November of that year.[24] Wang became the chairperson of EAI in 2007 when the institute was relocated to the Bukit Timah campus.[25] Wang's nostalgic recollections of the BTC were recorded in Zheng and Phua's co-edited volume:

> As you can see, for me, it is this Bukit Timah campus that excites me and triggers memories of the beautiful moments and bitter fights that linger on in my mind. This was where we studied, made friends and hopefully courted out wives. As many of you know, I was one of the successful ones.[26]

In terms of both personal anecdotes as well as his visionary venture for EAI, Wang's assumption of leadership at EAI made an impression on senior scholars around the world. None is as eloquent as eminent East Asian-ist Professor Ezra F Vogel when he described Wang's role during this period:

> In 1997, Gungwu took over the fledgling East Asian Institute of Singapore, originally founded with the hope of providing a moral underpinning for modern government, that had begun to define a new mission of studying economic developments. Gungwu helped to develop a new mission, of bringing historical breadth to bear in understanding mainland China.[27]

---

[24] John Wong, Aw Beng Teck and Lai Hongyi (eds), *Analysing China Commemorating EAI's 5th Anniversary*, p. 7.

[25] East Asian Institute (EAI), *Redefining Traditions Embracing Modernity Commemorating EAI's 15th Anniversary*, p. 4.

[26] Zheng Yongnian and Phua Kok Khoo (eds), *Wang Gungwu Educator and Scholar*, p. 205.

[27] Ezra Vogel, "Foreword" in Asad-ul Iqbal Latif, *Wang Gungwu: Junzi Scholar-Gentleman in Conversation with Asad-Ul Iqbal Latif* (Singapore: ISEAS Publishing, 2010), p. x.

The uniqueness of EAI is highlighted by Wang who pointed out that "EAI is the only research institute in Southeast Asia that focuses on the study of contemporary China and East Asia".[28] Under Wang's directorship, the institute widened its purview from Confucian studies to contemporary Chinese development and regional relations with its neighbours.[29] Wang's director job was by no means easy as China was only just integrating into the world economy and establishing official contact with the Chinese government and gaining access to conduct research in China required relationship-building. Eventually, this process was aided by Singapore's friendly relations with China and official establishment of diplomatic relations in 1990.[30]

Other achievements were also mentioned by Vogel, including the ability of Wang's leadership in attracting promising mainland Chinese scholars who were able to generate "crisp clear reports" based on their deep knowledge of contemporary Chinese development and macro issues.[31] The achievements were similarly lauded by Professor Tommy Koh, Singapore's Ambassador-at-Large, who noted that Wang's leadership "put the EAI on the world's map of leading think-tanks on modern China".[32]

---

[28] John Wong, Aw Beng Teck and Lai Hongyi (eds), *Analysing China Commemorating EAI's 5th Anniversary*, p. 6.

[29] East Asian Institute (EAI), *Redefining Traditions Embracing Modernity Commemorating EAI's 15th Anniversary*, p. 4.

[30] East Asian Institute (EAI), *Redefining Traditions Embracing Modernity Commemorating EAI's 15th Anniversary*, p. 4.

[31] Ezra Vogel, "Foreword" in Asad-ul Iqbal Latif, *Wang Gungwu Junzi Scholar-Gentleman in Conversation with Asad-Ul Iqbal Latif*, pp. x–xi.

[32] Asad-ul Iqbal Latif, *Wang Gungwu Junzi Scholar-Gentleman in Conversation with Asad-Ul Iqbal Latif*, p. xvi.

(EAI was ranked as one of the top five think tanks in the world by a US-based outfit with the results announced through the University of Pennsylvania, more on this in a later section.) The EAI informational brochure produced in 2010 also indicated that the institute had completed two non-profit consultancy projects including a Suzhou Industrial Park study carried out on behalf of the Ministry of Trade and Industry (MTI) in 2002 and on Hong Kong's 1997 return to mainland China, published in 1998.[33]

John Wong. Professor John Wong is another important individual whose earlier work was intertwined with the foundational origins of EAI. His administration and management experience in EAI has become synonymous with the institute itself. Wong became a specialist on China in the 1960s and, according to Hsuan Owyang, Wong was the receiver and successor of Goh's ideas about China watching or Sinology when he was director of IEAPE.[34] Wong's pressures (and learning experiences) in working with Goh were understandable since the latter received a first class honours degree in economics with a PhD in 1956 from the London School of Economics, Wong's alma mater, and was the de facto architect of Singapore's economy, a former deputy prime minister, minister of education and chairman of the Monetary Authority of Singapore.

Wong's fateful engagement with EAI started with a phone call from the personal assistant of Goh and the

---

[33] East Asian Institute, Singapore, East Asian Institute (Singapore: EAI), 2010, p. 12.
[34] Hsuan Owyang, "Speech by Mr Hsuan Owyang, Chairman, EAI Management Board EAI's 5th Anniversary Lectures 17 July 2002, Mandarin Hotel Your Excellencies", p. 3.

rest was history.[35] The two men then had the defining conversation which shifted EAI's future focus from philosophies and studies of the classics to contemporary Chinese knowledge-building. The intricacies of building up contemporary China knowledge was well-understood by Wong and he became the full-time director of IEAP in 1990,[36] then IEAPE and then research director of EAI.[37] In terms of textual collection, IEAP under Wong started on its documentary accumulation of knowledge through building up an inventory of official yearbooks, books and journals on contemporary China, which became the largest and most comprehensive library in this subject matter in Southeast Asia.[38] This achievement propelled Singapore to become a major centre of contemporary China studies in the region.

As a scholar, the challenges that Wong faced was enormous intellectually as he needed to incorporate non-economic perspectives into his training as an economist, something that resonated with Goh. He engaged in rigorous debates with major scholars in China studies, including the important debate over cultural determinism. In 2014, Shin Chueiling wrote a detailed article on Wong's methodology and research in studying the

---

[35] John Wong, "Goh Keng Swee and Contemporary China Studies in Singapore", a chapter in this volume.

[36] Zheng, Yongnian and John Wong (eds), *Goh Keng Swee on China Selected Essays*, p. 1.

[37] John Wong, "Goh Keng Swee and Contemporary China Studies in Singapore", a chapter in this volume; and Zheng, Yongnian and John Wong (eds), *Goh Keng Swee on China Selected Essays*, p. 1.

[38] John Wong, "Goh Keng Swee and Contemporary China Studies in Singapore", a chapter in this volume.

Chinese economy and, in it, Shin made three important points.[39] (This article by Shin Chueiling was published in the leading area studies journal *East Asia*.) Firstly, Shin argued that Wong's research is pragmatic and reflect practical contexts and constantly changing external environmental factors.[40] Secondly, Shin argues that this element of pragmatism is reflected in EAI as a research practice. Shin's research as well as interview with Wong himself indicated that EAI's research direction is also a reflection of the dynamically changing environment:

> ... each stage of the institute was given a different research assignment, based on the need to shift the focus of Singapore's China policy. The IEAP period, for example, emphasized the study of Confucian thought, when the Singaporean government — which had chosen to westernize the country for quick development — learned from its East Asian neighbors the merits of Confucian philosophy in modernization and thus encouraged Confucian thought to maintain stability in the 1970s and 1980s.[41]

Therefore, EAI and its predecessors have provided practical and applicable information to the state. This was the third main point made by Shin. He argues that Singapore is the point of departure for Wong's research, thus his study of China and EAI research output have a

---

[39] Shin Chueiling, "Understanding Chinese Economy Accurately-John Wong and His China Research", 18 June 2014 in *East Asia* (2014) 31 (Spring Science + Business Media Dordrecht, 2014), pp. 157–169.

[40] Shin Chueiling, "Understanding Chinese Economy Accurately-John Wong and His China Research", p. 163.

[41] Shin Chueiling, "Understanding Chinese Economy Accurately-John Wong and His China Research", p. 167.

Singapore-centred approach and the first two points were subsets of this methodology.

Through his engagement with other scholars and his painstaking efforts at physical facilities construction, Wong had to manage both infrastructure as well as building up knowledge base and human talents in the early days of the institute as the management executive of a young institute that was growing to be a major force in contemporary China studies in the region and then the world.[42] Wong as a professionally trained economist also had to make the transition from academic approaches to analyses (which he retained) to learning the ropes of policy research and writing as well (a skill that he soon mastered and acquired under the tutelage of Goh).[43] When EAI was established, Wong became its research director, having written over 80 policy reports for the Singapore government by that time, authored 33 books, 400 articles and chapters on China and other East Asian economies.[44] According to Hsuan Owyang, Wong's ideas were for EAI "to provide a good mix of politics, economics and international relations to cater to different audiences and different expectations".[45] In this way, Wong is an interpreter for both Eastern and Western audiences, filling in the informational gaps at an

---

[42] The detailed fascinating story of the Goh-Wong interactions and dialogues are detailed in the chapter on this subject matter in this volume written by Wong.

[43] John Wong, "Goh Keng Swee and Contemporary China Studies in Singapore", a chapter in this volume.

[44] Zheng Yongnian and John Wong (eds), *Goh Keng Swee on China Selected Essays*, p. v.

[45] Husn Owyang, *From Wall Street to Bukit Merah* (Singapore and KL: Times Books International, 1998), pp. 181–182.

exceptional historical period when there was a lack of information about China during the Cold War.

Passing the Baton

Wong retired in 2009 and by then, EAI had published over 500 *Background Briefs*, a testament to Wong's tireless efforts.[46] After his retirement, he remained as the professorial fellow and academic adviser at EAI, facilitating other young scholars' access to his experience and accumulated knowledge. Other than quantitative output, Wong's achievements should also be measured against Singapore's political context during the Cold War when there were ideological struggles between the capitalist and free world camp versus the socialist camp. The challenges faced are detailed in Wong's chapter on Goh Keng Swee in this volume. While Wong managed internal procedures for the smooth running of the institute, Wang dealt with externalities of establishing relations with Chinese scholars and officialdom. Wang retired as EAI director in 2007 and became the chairperson of its management board, and one of his last few major projects in the same year was to organise the bilingual EAI's 10th Anniversary international conferences.[47]

Though the Wang-Wong team has passed the baton to a new generation of scholars and management, Wang remains as the institute's chairman (affectionately termed

---

[46] John Wong, "Goh Keng Swee and Contemporary China Studies in Singapore", a chapter in this volume.

[47] Zheng Yongnian and Phua Kok Khoo (eds), *Wang Gungwu Educator and Scholar*, p. 384.

as the "chairman-at-large" by others in the policy-making circle)[48] and Wong as the professorial fellow and senior adviser (Wong's counsel and guidance remain deeply beneficial to rising young Chinese and local scholars). Their advice and guidance are sought by the successor generation of scholars led by Zheng Yongnian. Wong and Zheng also teamed up to edit and produce a volume on Goh Keng Swee's writings in 2013, an optimal choice given that both of them are familiar with Goh's written ideas.[49]

Zheng Yongnian. Professor Zheng is the second generation-leader of EAI who graduated with a BA and an MA from the Peking University and a PhD from Ivy League Princeton. He was a recipient of the prestigious Social Science Research Council-MacArthur Foundation Fellowship (1995–1997) and John D and Catherine T MacArthur Foundation Fellowship (2003–2004).[50] Aside from academic achievements, Zheng had practitioner's experience as the consultant to the United Nations Development Programme on China's rural development and democracy.[51]

---

[48] There is some truth to this as Zheng and Phua wrote in their volume, "In Singapore, Wang is concurrently the chairman of three institutions, namely the East Asian institute, the Institute of Southeast Asian Studies and the Lee Kuan Yew School of Public Policy. In addition, he is a member of 11 other boards and institutions in Singapore and over 30 boards of overseas institutions and international journals". (Source: Zheng Yongnian and Phua Kok Khoo [eds], *Wang Gungwu Educator and Scholar*, p. vi).

[49] Zheng Yongnian and John Wong (eds), *Goh Keng Swee on China Selected Essays*, p. 3.

[50] Zheng Yongnian and Phua Kok Khoo (eds), *Wang Gungwu Educator and Scholar*, p. xi.

[51] Zheng Yongnian and Phua Kok Khoo (eds), *Wang Gungwu Educator and Scholar*, p. xi.

In Wong's memoirs of Goh, Zheng's membership in EAI in 1996 was explained against the context of the lack of PRC Chinese scholars with appropriate qualifications from top universities in the United States at that time. Zheng was recruited as the institute's first PRC academician with a PhD in political science, a historical milestone in itself.[52] This is reflective of the evolution of EAI's history, from Confucianist roots in the humanities to the Goh-Wang-Wong team's emphasis on contemporary China and finally to contemporary China scholarship under the directorship of a US-trained Chinese scholar. The institute serves the vital national interests of Singapore, as well as maintains the bridge in Sino-Singaporean exchanges to eventually become a regionally and globally recognised think tank for academic exchange and policy studies. In EAI's fifth anniversary commemorative book, Zheng was featured as one of EAI's Chinese experts on politics who was "widely sought for their views on China by the local media".[53]

Starting off as a research fellow in 1997 as a young scholar, Zheng became EAI's director in 2008/9. His leadership marked a new dynamic phase in contemporary China studies against the backdrop of the rise of China and its ascent from a developing economy to the world's third largest and then second largest economy in 2010 and potentially the world's largest in purchasing power parity (PPP) term. Just as complex as China's developmental fast-growth phases, this rising status also parallels a new debate in

---

[52] John Wong, "Goh Keng Swee and Contemporary China Studies in Singapore", a chapter in this volume.
[53] John Wong, Aw Beng Teck and Lai Hongyi (eds), *Analysing China Commemorating EAI's 5th Anniversary*, p. 15.

intellectual and policy-making circles which is the narrative of a "China path" that has attracted global attention.[54] Zheng is in a unique position to analyse this phenomenon as a global citizen, a Chinese national and a Singapore resident. His ability to analyse China through a globalised perspective and US-trained academic tradition serves as a conduit for conveying Chinese cultural nuances to a Western and global audience. With his Chinese roots, Zheng is grounded in cultural understanding of China from a China-centred viewpoint. In fact, Zheng may represent the pioneering trend of future generations of EAI scholars who are immersed in their cultural heritage, trained in the West and observing China from the platform of Singapore as a resident and global citizen.

Simultaneously, Zheng's residence in Singapore provides the objective distance for China watching while staying relevant to Singapore's policy-making circles (entrenched as part of the institute's mission since Goh's era). Under Zheng's directorship, Wang's chairmanship and Wong's senior advisory role (a three generational "dream team"), EAI achieved remarkable results when it was ranked fifth in the Asia-Pacific in the 2013 Global Go To Think Tank Survey.[55] The ranking was announced on 22 January 2014

---

[54] East Asian Institute (EAI), *Redefining Traditions Embracing Modernity Commemorating EAI's 15th Anniversary*, p. 5.

[55] James G McGann, "East Asian Institute Ranks Fifth in Asia and the Pacific Region in 2013 Global Go To Think Tank Survey" in the Gotothinktank. com website, available at http://gotothinktank.com/dev1/wp-content/uploads/2014/01/GoToReport2013.pdf, accessed 11 October 2014; "East Asian Institute (EAI) is placed fifth overall in the Asia and the Pacific category (which excludes China, India, Japan and South Korea) of the 2013 Global Go To Think Tank Survey's annual rankings".

by the University of Pennsylvania's Think Tanks and Civil Societies Programme at the United Nations University and the World Bank in Washington DC.[56]

Other instrumental figures. There were other instrumental historical figures in EAI's formation, which is by itself a story of continuity and discontinuity. According to Owyang, EAI inherited the IEAPE's library resources and database as well as funding endowment.[57] In his memoirs, Owyang described the EAI library as "the best library on contemporary China in the region".[58] As at June 2014, EAI had a huge collection of books (54,119 volumes and 39,537 titles), 644 yearbooks, 272 subscribed journals, 19 newspapers, as well as a microfilm and microfiche collection.[59] Owyang's biographical writing dedicated three pages of important information about EAI in his memoir. In his writing, Owyang differentiated EAI from its predecessor IEAPE, arguing that EAI is a component of the National University of Singapore while IEAPE was a private firm and the audience for EAI's publications were wider in scope compared to that of IEAPE which fed its output only to the cabinet, senior public servants and a

---

[56] James G McGann, "East Asian Institute Ranks Fifth in Asia and the Pacific Region in 2013 Global Go To Think Tank Survey" in the Gotothinktank. com website, available at http://gotothinktank.com/dev1/wp-content/uploads/2014/01/GoToReport2013.pdf, accessed 11 October 2014.

[57] Owyang Hsuan, "Speech by Mr Hsuan Owyang, Chairman, EAI Management Board EAI's 5th Anniversary Lectures 17 July 2002, Mandarin Hotel Your Excellencies", p. 2.

[58] Owyang Hsuan, *From Wall Street to Bukit Merah*, p. 182.

[59] East Asian Institute, Singapore, East Asian Institute (Singapore: EAI), 2010, p. 26.

small circle of subscribers.[60] Owyang described the objectives of the EAI as the following:[61]

1. to conduct research on areas pertaining to East Asian development and, in particular, contemporary China;
2. to participate in ad hoc research projects proposed by the institute, ministries and other statutory boards; and
3. to participate and assist in the organisation of promotional and exchange programmes with similar regional institutions as well as regional and international conferences and workshops on East Asian issues, especially contemporary development in China.

Owyang described the makeup of EAI's management committee during his tenure as chairperson. He mentioned that EAI is staffed by a few Singapore ministerial permanent secretaries and a few deans from the National University of Singapore. Adding some names to this distinguished list of office-holders that Owyang listed are the National University of Singapore and its own leaders, Professor Tan Chorh Chuan and predecessors Professors Lim Pin and Shih Choon Fong. Their facilitation of EAI activities had made its success possible and practicable. Shih described the founding of EAI as "NUS's first university-level non-natural-science research institute".[62] As an autonomous entity within the university system, it enjoys the University's activities and the lively dialogues and discussions of the campus' scholarly denizens.

---

[60] Hsuan Owyang, *From Wall Street to Bukit Merah*, p. 181.
[61] Hsuan Owyang, *From Wall Street to Bukit Merah*, p. 181.
[62] John Wong, Aw Beng Teck and Lai Hongyi (eds), *Analysing China Commemorating EAI's 5th Anniversary*, p. 4.

Scholarly Perceptions

In addition to being an observer of historical events, Wang has the additional viewpoint of watching China from the perspective of an "overseas Chinese" at a time when there were vigorous debates and sensitivities about the terminologies of "overseas Chinese" itself (for detailed discussions and debates about the concept of "overseas Chinese" and its differentiation from the term "Chinese overseas", please refer to Wang Gungwu's *The Chinese Overseas*[63]). In fact, the idea (and perception) of overseas Chinese scholars studying China has not gone unnoticed in the Chinese-speaking (sometimes known as 'Greater China', another term of contention) world. This applies to academic evaluations of EAI and its management's achievements as well. Taiwan-based scholar Chen Changhong wrote an important article on Wang, Wong and Zheng's (Chen described them as "overseas Chinese") contribution to the study of China and Singaporean governmental agencies' reliance on their insights.[64] Putting the complex debate of what constitutes "overseas Chinese" aside, the paper centred discussions of these three Sinologists in the complex concept of

[63] For detailed discussions about the concept of overseas Chinese, please refer to Wang Gungwu, *The Chinese Overseas* (Cambridge, MA: Harvard University Press, 2002). The historical context of the PRC"s "*huaqiao*" policies is also briefly discussed in Leo Suryadinata's publications, for e.g. Leo Suraydinata, "A New Orientation in China's Policy towards Chinese Overseas? Beijing Olympic Games fervour as a Case Study", in *CHC Bulletin*, November 2008, Issue 12, p. 3, available at http://chc.ntu.edu.sg/Bulletin/Documents/CHC_Bulletin12.pdf, accessed 15 October 2014.
[64] Chen Changhong, "The Chineseness of Overseas Chinese Scholars and Their Institutions — Case Study of Professor Wang GungWu, John Wong and Zheng Yongnian of EAI" in Development Studies Annual Conference, p. 1.

"Chineseness (*huarenxing*)" to discuss how life experiences and one's environmental upbringing and parental heritage contextualise and colour perceptions of the concept of "China" or "Chineseness".[65]

One may not totally agree with Chen's use, deployment or conceptualisations of "immigrant", "homeland", "diaspora" or "diasporic theory",[66] but the fact that he raised these terms and debates in the context of studying EAI and Wang/Wong/Zheng's ideas implies that the contributions of EAI's leadership have drawn important attention from the scholarly world. Wang's, Wong's and Zheng's ideas are in their own ways intellectual responses to the external impact of historical context. The ideas represent different birthplaces, upbringings, educational influences and historical life experiences.

Yet, at the same time, Chen argues that there are dialectics at play here. Even as external environmental forces shape personal judgements, evaluations and sense of objectivity, Chen's interpretation of Wang's ideas is that he sees the concept of "Chineseness" in a state of perpetual dynamic changes.[67] And therefore because of this constantly evolving nature, the intensity of the concept of "Chineseness" can "strengthen" or "dilute" according to

---

[65] Chen Changhong, "The Chineseness of Overseas Chinese Scholars and Their Institutions — Case Study of Professor Wang GungWu, John Wong and Zheng Yongnian of EAI", p. 2.

[66] Chen Changhong, "The Chineseness of Overseas Chinese Scholars and Their Institutions — Case Study of Professor Wang GungWu, John Wong and Zheng Yongnian of EAI", p. 3.

[67] Chen Changhong, "The Chineseness of Overseas Chinese Scholars and Their Institutions — Case Study of Professor Wang GungWu, John Wong and Zheng Yongnian of EAI", p. 5.

contextual factors.[68] The idea of "us" versus "them" in Chen's article[69] is often articulated by Wong in his description of the interpreter role. Wong sees himself as an intermediary between East and West, interpreting ideas relevant to the Singaporean context. In discussion of EAI and its leadership, Chen's ideas draw similarities and differences with Shin Chueiling's ideas.

The similarities lie in two areas. Both highlighted the importance of contextual studies and EAI itself is an institution that evolved with the rise of China and Singapore's nation-building process to stay relevant. Both Shin and Chen agree on the multiple identities that EAI and its leadership encompass, incorporating "Chineseness (emphasised by Chen)", "Singapore-centredness (as emphasised by Shin)" and "East-West hybridisation (as emphasised by Wong in his analogy of an interpreter role)". However there are also differences in scholarly ideas between Chen and Shin. Chen argues that both Sinology and EAI's founding scholars constantly work with changing trends in Sinology while Shin highlights the constant Singapore-centredness of Wong's research in parallel with institutional needs. Chen's article articulates the lack of a set of core ideas in Chinese studies and the need to search for commonalities in building up knowledge for the subject matter while Shin opined that EAI and its administrators

---

[68] Chen Changhong, "The Chineseness of Overseas Chinese Scholars and Their Institutions — Case Study of Professor Wang GungWu, John Wong and Zheng Yongnian of EAI", p. 5.

[69] Chen Changhong, "The Chineseness of Overseas Chinese Scholars and Their Institutions — Case Study of Professor Wang GungWu, John Wong and Zheng Yongnian of EAI", p. 3.

centre their activities on Singapore's national interests as research priorities.

Ultimately, both accounts are providing different perspectives of the same institution of EAI and its leadership. EAI and Wang/Wong/Zheng are simultaneously representing scholarships of changing ideas about China and its developments while centring their research on the practical task of informing both the Singaporean government as well as the scholarly community at large about China. In other words, Wang/Wong/Zheng and EAI have multiple identities as objective scholars, neutral interpreters, Singapore-centred Sinologists, cultural intermediaries, experts in an ideologically neutralised environment and pragmatic administrators.

Real World Application

According to the 2010 EAI corporate booklet, the institute is extending its research efforts to cover Japan and Korea even as it focuses on China (including Hong Kong and Taiwan).[70] In fact, the institute now effectively covers a region-wide northeast Asian portfolio. There are more continuity than changes in EAI's future as Wong argues in his chapter in this volume that EAI scholars strive for scholarly neutrality (non-PRC and non-Western in orientation) in order to make written briefs more useful for the Singapore government. This was a tradition right from the beginning when Wong penned the first report in the *IEAP China News Analysis No. 1* issued on 3 January 1991.

---

[70] East Asian Institute, Singapore, East Asian Institute (Singapore: EAI), 2010, pp. 2–3.

Just as EAI and its leadership have evolved, Singapore's interaction with China have also evolved accordingly (or as Zheng puts it "constantly evolving according to changes" 一直在随着大环境的变化而变化). In the past, there were inadequate information and news about China. With time, China and its information release have become more open. Now more Singaporeans are working there. In 2012, according to the local media *The Straits Times*, 20,000 Singaporeans were working in China, the fourth largest group overseas which is fast catching up with its top three destinations.[71] Therefore, EAI is no longer the exclusive source of information and news about China. These are external factors that are likely to shape the future of EAI. However the rise of China is also a complex event for Singaporeans with their own cultural nuances and political sensitivities that are likely to contribute to the next lap of the EAI evolution.

Last words. In the practitioners/policy sphere, researches have resulted in practical advice and commentaries to a large number of stakeholders, including those in the media, government and business sectors. Singapore's stake in the continued relevance and importance of the institute are well-articulated through its current management staff. "One of Singapore's overriding objectives is to stay relevant to China's growth," said EAI Assistant Director Lye Liang Fook; he continues, "If this is the case, then it is in Singapore's interest to constantly find opportunities to

---

[71] Theresa Tan, "200,000 S'poreans living abroad", *The Straits Times*, 14 October 2012, unpaginated, available at http://lkyspp.nus.edu.sg/ips/wp-content/uploads/sites/2/2013/06/ST_200000-Singaporeans-living-abroad_141012.pdf, accessed 15 October 2014.

collaborate with China to derive win-win benefits."[72] Lye's words and emphasis echo those of former Minister of Trade and Industry George Yeo's thinking on the fifth anniversary of EAI:

> China is both a huge challenge and an historic opportunity. If we respond correctly, Singapore will be able to ride on China's growing prosperity. If we don't our lives will become much more difficult. The EAI plays an important role in helping us formulate our responses.[73]

These two views knit together a sense of continuity and mission for EAI's policy advisory journey.

Prepared by Lim Tai Wei on behalf of EAI (The author would like to express his gratitude to Professor Zheng Yongnian, Professor John Wong, Dr Yang Mu and Ms Jessica Loon for their materials and feedback).

---

[72] Rachel Chang, "Straits Times: 3 possible locations for third Sino-S'pore project", undated on the MFA website in the Ministry of Foreign Affairs website, available at http://www.mfa.gov.sg/content/mfa/media_centre/singapore_headlines/2014/201408/headlines_20140808.html, accessed 13 October 2014.

[73] John Wong, Aw Beng Teck and Lai Hongyi (eds), *Analysing China Commemorating EAI's 5th Anniversary*, p. 3.

Goh Keng Swee and Contemporary China Studies in Singapore

John Wong

Professorial Fellow and Academic Adviser,
East Asian Institute, Singapore

Introduction

Goh Keng Swee was formerly deputy prime minister and minister for defence of Singapore. Shortly after his retirement from politics in 1985, Goh became a special economic adviser to China's State Council on the opening up of China's coastal cities and on tourism development (1985–1990). He founded the Institute of East Asian Philosophies (IEAP) in 1983 to promote Confucian ethics for the Moral Education Programme of Singapore's schools.

In 1990 John Wong was appointed by Goh as director of IEAP. The research direction of IEAP was changed from Confucian and Religious studies to the research on the political, economic and social development of contemporary China. In 1992, IEAP was renamed the Institute of East Asian Political Economy (IEAPE), which was subsequently closed down in 1997 to become East Asian Institute (EAI).

This chapter is adapted from Chapter 9 of the book, *Gok Keng Swee: A Legacy of Public Service*, edited by Emrys CHEW and Chong Guan KWA. (Singapore, NTU and World Scientific, 2012).

I. Confucian Studies in Singapore

Goh Keng Swee was a central figure in Singapore's Confucianism campaign in the 1980s. What had prompted him to embrace Confucianism so enthusiastically in the first place? I did not have the opportunity of working under him when he first started his mission of introducing Confucian studies to Singapore. Nor was I a staff at the Institute of East Asian Philosophies (IEAP) at the time when it was fully devoted to the pursuit of Confucian studies.

When I started work at IEAP in late 1990, I made arrangements for the institute's Confucian scholars to return to their original home organisations. My other main job during the transition period was to arrange for the institute's books and papers on East Asian philosophies and religions (an extremely valuable collection, indeed) to be transferred to the National University of Singapore (NUS) Central Library on a permanent loan basis. At that time, IEAP was already in the process of building up, very aggressively, its own collection of official yearbooks, books and journals on contemporary China. Today, the collection on contemporary China stands out as the best and most comprehensive in the whole of Southeast Asia.

Back to the issue of Confucian studies, I will use my own past research to narrate the "rise and fall" of the Confucianism Campaign in Singapore, with anecdotes from my recollection of casual conversations with Goh over this subject, to piece together a more consistent account of Goh's involvement and his changing attitudes towards this subject.[1]

---

[1] My work on this subject yielded two publications. See John Wong and Aline Wong, "Confucian Values as A Social Framework for Singapore's Economic Development", in Chung-Hua Institution for Economic Research, Conference

Confucian Ethics and East Asian Development

Mainstream economists are always uncomfortable with employing non-economic factors to explain economic development, avoiding in particular the cultural explanation of economic development. At the same time, pure economic theory alone cannot adequately handle the complex process of economic development. Thus, it stands to reason that apart from the primary economic factors of capital and technology, people's attitudes and beliefs, and their social relations and cultural systems "must have strongly affected the working of those primary economic forces", as one well-known (or notable) development economist put it.[2]

Goh himself held similar views: "There is now clear recognition among economists that economic growth involves more than economic variables. Gunnar Myrdal's monumental *Asian Drama* makes the most thorough and explicit study of non-economic factors which have a bearing on economic growth. However, Myrdal's plea for a new set of economic principles applicable to the situation of less developed countries has largely been ignored. The economist stands fast by his principle of doctrinal purity".[3]

In the late 1970s, following the economic rise of Japan and the four East Asian Newly Industrialising Economies

Proceeding Series No. 13, "Conference on Confucianism and Economic Development in East Asia" (29 to 31 May 1999); and John Wong, "Promoting Confucianism for Socioeconomic Development: The Singapore Experience", in Tu Wei-ming (ed.), *Confucian Traditions in East Asian Modernity* (Cambridge, Massachusetts: Harvard University Press, 1996).

[2] Bert F. Hoselitz, "Economic Growth and Development: Non-economic Factors in Economic Factors", *American Economic Review* (May 1957).

[3] Goh Keng Swee, *The Economics of Modernization and Other Essays* (Singapore: Asia Pacific Press, 1972), p. 2.

(NIEs) of South Korea, Taiwan, Hong Kong and Singapore, many broad-minded development economists and social commentators started to explore the underlying non-economic causes of East Asia's economic dynamism. To the extent that these East Asian economies all share mainstream cultural traditions of China as embodied in Confucianism, it was argued that Confucian values and similar cultural traits must be an important exogenous factor for East Asia's economic success. In fact, Herman Kahn was among the first to emphatically link the economic success of the East Asian economies to the cultural factors operating in these "Neo-Confucian societies".[4]

However, serious debate on the issue of Confucian values and economic development was started by two eminent "overseas Japanese" economists: Michio Morishima, a specialist on Marxian economics at LSE, and Harry Oshima, a development economist from the United States working at the University of the Philippines. While Morishima attributed Japan's economic success to the tenets of the Japanese version of Confucianism, Oshima argued that the more rational, pragmatic and utilitarian Confucian culture was inherently more conducive to modern economic growth than the social value systems of either Hinduism or Mahayana Buddhism, and hence the clear difference in the economic performance between East Asia and South Asia.[5]

---

[4] Herman Kahn, *World Economic Development: 1979 and Beyond* (London: Croom Helm, 1979).

[5] Michio Morishima, *Why Has Japan Succeeded: Western Technology and Japanese Ethos* (Cambridge: Cambridge University Press, 1982). Harry Oshima, *Economic Growth in Monsoon Asia: A Comparative Survey* (Tokyo: Tokyo University Press, 1987).

From today's standpoint, Oshima's argument comes close to cultural determinism, which is clearly unacceptable to mainstream social scientists. All cultures are capable of carrying out industrialisation and all societies can be modernised. Indeed, the subsequent economic take-off in Malaysia and Thailand has forcefully demonstrated that Islam and Buddhism are equally conducive to economic development.

Even back in the days when many commentators were hotly debating the role of Confucianism in East Asian development, most mainstream social scientists were cautious about such cultural explanations. Many took the view that the role of Confucianism in this process is at most "necessary, but not sufficient". One might argue that Confucian ethics, in promoting personal thrift and hard work, is conducive to productivity growth and capital formation. Its emphasis on education and learning, all growth-inducing social forces, is good for manpower development and human capital formation. However there are also other cultural traits associated with Confucianism that are not so conducive to economic growth.

More serious is the methodological issue. Lawrence Lau has argued that any cultural explanation, such as an attempt to pinpoint Confucianism as a fundamental cause of East Asia's economic success, amounts to a tautological argument in the sense that it merely repeats the same observed facts in a different way, with little or no new explanatory power.[6] Hence, many mainstream economists

---

[6] Lawrence J. Lau, "A Comparative Analysis of Economic Development Experience in Chinese Societies", paper presented at the International Symposium on Economic Development in Chinese Societies, Models and Experiences organised by the Hong Kong Economic Association, 18 to 20 December 1986.

remain sceptical about this issue when they come to formal economic arguments.

I believe Goh's position was quite mixed. As a good economist with a rigorous and analytical mind, plus a strong methodological background based on the LSE tradition of hypothesis testing and falsification of hypotheses (contributing to his stance that one cannot prove anything in social sciences), he would feel uneasy with such fuzzy logic underlying the cultural explanation. At the same time, he was aware that economic development is such a complex, multi-dimensional process that pure economic theory often fails to provide a complete explanation for its success or failure.

Some development economists have made normative arguments to explain certain development phenomena. The noted Oxford economist I. M. D. Little, in examining the successful development experiences of East Asia, crisply concluded that "everything can be attributed to good policies and the people".[7] What is a "good" policy? Clearly, this is not a positive statement. I think Goh would also argue in the same way as Little. Goh had the gut feeling that many traditional cultural traits are good for business success and conducive to economic development.

In fact, it needs to be emphasised that neither Goh nor any other Singapore leader has openly attributed Singapore's successful economic development to the working of Confucian ethics. From these observations, it is clear that

---

[7] I. M. D. Little, "The Experience and Causes of Rapid Labour-intensive Development in Korea, Taiwan Province, Hong Kong, and Singapore and the Possibilities of Emulation", in A. R. Khan (ed.), *Export-Led Industrialization and Development* (Geneva: International Labour Organization, 1981), p. 43.

Goh's promotion of Confucian studies was not for economic reasons, but primarily for certain social purposes.

The Confucianism Campaign

By the late 1970s, the Singapore economy had already achieved take-off, with sustained high growth and full employment. As in today's China, a long period of rapid economic growth in Singapore had brought about rapid social change while the resulting economic prosperity had also started to erode traditional social values. This was especially true of the younger generation, who would generally equate economic modernisation with Westernisation, with some even adopting what was then referred to as the "permissive lifestyle of the West". The problem was considered more serious for Singapore because Singaporeans mostly communicate in English as their first language, thereby subjected to rapid, direct exposure to Western values and thinking from Western media and television programmes. Other East Asian societies like Taiwan and South Korea experienced similar problems but were less acute because their use of national language provided some kind of insulation.

In an interview with a Taiwanese journalist, then Prime Minister Lee Kuan Yew confirmed his concerns as follows:[8]

> I think we will face a serious problem because of the constant assault on our core values, like attitudes between men and women, husband and wife, father and children, attitudes between citizens and the government. Singaporeans watched so much of Western, especially American television that they

---

[8] *The Straits Times*, 3 January 1989.

may begin to feel that is the norm, that is the standard. And we may move into that standard unconsciously.

Lee was clearly referring to the Confucian ethics as embodied in the "Five Principal Relations" (Mencius' *san-gang wu-chang* 三纲五常). But long before that, Singaporean leaders had already decided to strengthen the moral education of the young in schools by inculcating more Asian values in them as possible ballast against the daily assault from Western values. This explains why, shortly after taking charge of the Ministry of Education (January 1979), Goh released the "Goh Report" on education, which, among other things, recommended Moral Education as a replacement for the existing Education for Living and Civics courses in schools.

Initially, the Moral Education programme was supposed to be purely ethical rather than religious, stressing such universal values as honesty and integrity. It was soon realised that it would be more effective to teach these ethics within a certain religious context since many mission schools had already been doing this for their religious study courses. In fact, it would be hard to teach Malay students moral values in isolation from Islamic teachings. Thus, it was decided in January 1982 that moral education and religious studies would be consolidated as "Religious Knowledge", comprising any one of Singapore's four major religions of Buddhism, Christianity, Islam and Hinduism, plus "World Religions" as an alternative for non-believers and agnostics. The much-heralded Confucianism was added as the sixth option a month later.

Soon after the teaching of Confucianism became official, Goh started to invite a group of eminent Chinese Confucian scholars working in the United States, including Professor Tu Wei-Ming of Harvard and Professor Yu Ying-Shih of Yale, to Singapore to advise the government on how to select the Confucian values that would still be relevant to a modern society like Singapore. Public lectures were also organised for them to explain and popularise Confucianism to the general public. More specifically, some of these Confucian scholars were asked to help prepare suitable curricula for the teaching of Confucian ethics in schools. Furthermore, the Institute of East Asian Philosophies was set up in June 1983 for foreign Confucian scholars to promote and re-interpret Confucianism.

The introduction of Confucianism into the school curriculum clearly marked the climax of the whole Moral Education exercise. But this project was fraught with problems and resistance from the outset. Few would doubt that Lee Kuan Yew as prime minister and Goh Keng Swee as deputy prime minister were themselves convinced of the intrinsic virtue of Confucianism's social and cultural values. As these two top leaders threw their weight behind the campaign to promote Confucianism, it inevitably stirred up a lot of uneasiness among other non-Chinese ethnic groups. Worse still, many Singapore's English-educated Chinese were cool towards this campaign from the start, partly because of their lack of proper understanding of the Confucian philosophy. Some were simply turned off by such "Confucian vices" as nepotism, cronyism and subordination of women.

From the beginning, the government made it clear that Confucianism was promoted merely as personal ethics, not as a state ideology. But this had not prevented some unsympathetic Western journalists from using this issue to blacken the Singapore government for promoting Confucianism as a means to perpetuate its "authoritarian rule". Many Western liberals were also hostile to what they considered as a further attempt at social engineering.

However, the greatest setback to the campaign came from the declining support of Chinese students (and their parents). Several years after Goh had retired from active politics, a 1989 survey indicated that among 36,900 students at secondary three level who took the Religious Knowledge options, only 18 per cent opted for Confucian Ethics, compared to 44 per cent for Buddhist Studies, 21 per cent for Bible Knowledge and 13 per cent for Islamic Religious Knowledge. This meant that barely one-quarter of the total ethnic Chinese student population had taken up Confucian ethics. This must have been a great disappointment to the original promoters.

Among the reasons for the failure, it was later discovered, was that the Confucian Ethics course was just too demanding for Singapore students. It was hard for many of them without a strong command of the Chinese language to score high marks in the examination, especially compared to other religious courses. Much like the more recent debates over the teaching of the mother-tongue languages in schools, many students and their parents treated the course mainly as an examination subject, rather than appreciating its intrinsic social and cultural values in the long term. Furthermore, outside the classroom, Confucianism as a body of worldly wisdom without spiritual underpinnings could not compete against religions, which have well-established infrastructure like temples, churches and rituals.

In the meantime, the Confucianism campaign sparked off something of a religious revival in Singapore, with local adherents of both Buddhism and Christianity making fervent efforts at proselytisation. These developments alerted the government to the potential danger of arousing religious-ethnic tensions in a largely multicultural Singapore. It eventually led to the government's decision to wind down the Confucianism campaign. The great social experiment formally came to an end when the Religious Knowledge options were finally removed from the school curriculum.

How much was Goh a Confucianist?

As mentioned earlier, Goh at the beginning must have been attracted to Confucianism as a great ancient philosophy, finding many aspects of Confucian ethics as intrinsically good and useful social values for the people of Singapore. When this social experiment failed, he must have also been disappointed. Did this turn him off from Confucianism altogether? This issue needs to be studied at both the practical and intellectual levels.

Goh was known to many people as a very "practical" person. For many public policy decisions, he adopted a technocratic approach. He started the Confucianism campaign with great enthusiasm as he saw great social merits in doing this. He had probably underestimated the enormous political, social and cultural obstacles that were standing in the way of its implementation in multicultural Singapore. Thereafter, as he saw how such a campaign could stoke social and religious conflicts, he quickly called it off, as the potential political and social costs would outweigh the perceived benefits.

At the practical policy level, Goh might have grown disenchanted with Confucianism, particularly when it came to its applicability to Singapore. At the intellectual level, however, his attitude towards Confucianism was quite different. Confucian philosophy is profound and wide-ranging. A reasonable modern scholar would take an eclectic approach. He would intellectually embrace some aspects of Confucian ethics, but at the same time would also find others not relevant to the modern world.

For Confucianism to be employed as statecraft, China's rulers over the ages vowed to follow the principle of "government by virtue" (*yi-de wei-zheng* 以德为政). As Singapore is clearly ruled by law, Goh would certainly find this irrelevant for modern Singapore. It may be noted that China today is adopting double standards. While its present leadership has been stressing the importance of "rule of law" and "rule by law", they also advocate how the behaviour of leaders should also be guided by virtue (*de* 德).

At the same time, China's mandarin system, which is a product of Confucianism, appealed a lot to Goh. A Confucian scholar is not just a learned person, but also a highly moral and well-educated gentleman (*jun-zi* 君子). He also has the duty to become an official to serve the country (*Xue-er-you-ze-shi* 学而优则士) and this process is achieved through the competitive imperial examination system. Goh was certainly a great fan of such an elite-based civil service system, and he was known to have surrounded himself with many bright young scholars when he was at the Ministry of Defence and Ministry of Education. To him, a good official must have "brains" and "integrity". This is exactly what a Confucian mandarin ought to be.

In particular, Goh held in great esteem a few high Chinese officials in the late Qing period, which he considered the *crème de la crème* of China's "scholar-officials" in the true Confucian tradition. They include "scholar-generals" Zeng Guofan (曾国藩), who suppressed the Taiping Rebellion; Zuo Zongtang (左宗堂), who pacified Xinjiang; and the famous "scholar-diplomat" Li Hongzhang (李鸿章), who also initiated the Self-Strengthening Movement by selectively emulating certain Western practices (or the *Yangwu Yundong* 洋务运动).

Goh was also intrigued by the belated attempts of some late Qing officials to start industrialisation in China by setting up selective state-owned industries under *guan-du-shang-ban* (官督商办 or state supervision with commercial management). They include "scholar-entrepreneurs" Zhang Zhidong (张之洞) and Sheng Xuanhuai (盛宣怀). The early industrialisation efforts of the late Qing officials were not conspicuously successful, partly because of the unfavourable institutional environment prevailing in China at that time and partly due to their failure to separate the state (*guan*) from the market (*shang*).[9] According to Goh, the late Qing officials did not really understand the workings of the market. To him, a successful state enterprise

---

[9] For further detail, see Albert Feuerwerker, *China's Early Industrialization: Sheng Hsuan-huai (1844–1916) and Mandarin Enterprise* (Cambridge, Massachusetts: Harvard University Press, 1958).

must follow the key performance indicator of maximising profits as well as embracing open market competition. These are, in fact, the ground rules he set for many of Singapore's government-linked companies (GLCs) he had established.

To what extent, then, was Goh's admiration of these "scholar-officials" a self-image of himself? After all, he had done for Singapore many of the things that the Confucian "scholar-officials" had done for China. Certainly, Goh would not regard himself a Confucian scholar in any formal, academic sense, though he had acquired a lot of fundamental knowledge about Confucianism through reading the Confucian classics and discussions with various Chinese-American Confucian scholars he had invited to Singapore. But the Confucianism campaign certainly rubbed off a lot on him and he ended up being quite a Confucian-influenced gentleman himself.

In a very broad sense, many ethnic Chinese, both in China or living overseas, could claim to be "Confucians" or followers of Confucius even though they have never read any Confucian classics. This is because Confucianism, as an ethical system of norms and behaviour, has already permeated mainstream Chinese customs and rituals, which have been passed down from generation to generation through practice or oral transmission. Some sociologists refer to such daily Confucian practices as a form of "folk Confucianism" or "vulgar Confucianism".[10] What Goh subscribed to was more of the intellectual version of

---

[10] See Peter Berger and Hsin-Huang Michael Hsiao, *In Search of an East Asian Development Model* (New Jersey: Transactions Books, 1988), p. 19.

Confucianism, as embraced by the gentry and intelligentsia of old China.

II. "China Watching"

The Institute of East Asian Political Economy (IEAPE)

If Goh's attitude towards Confucian ethics was mixed, sometimes very positive and sometimes wavering, his approach to modern Chinese studies was nothing short of enthusiastic, much like a new convert's. When he decided to change the research direction of IEAP in 1990, he had already been in China for five years as an "official adviser" to the State Council's "Office of Special Economic Zones" under Vice Premier Gu Mu. Goh's job was to advise Gu on new policies and strategies to promote the further opening up of China's coastal cities. For this assignment, he travelled to China frequently, holding discussions with China's central and local government officials. He could then see firsthand what was happening in China, not just in Beijing and Shanghai, but in many other localities: they must have been eye-opening experiences, prompting him to learn more about China. Thereafter, he would progress from the "how" to the "why" of events on the ground, with his enquiring mind always seeking answers and solutions.

Furthermore, China in the second half of the 1980s was at the most critical phase of its economic reform. China started economic reform officially in 1979, first in the rural areas and the agricultural sector, with quick and successful results, laying a good foundation for the next phase of reform. The second phase, however, proved to be much more intractable when it was directed at the industrial sector in urban areas. Many transitional economies in Eastern Europe took a "Big Bang" approach to confront their reform problems in this area. Deng Xiaoping, in contrast, preferred a gradual approach through trial and error ("crossing the river by feeling the stones"). Though less disruptive, this gradualist reform strategy led China to a "half-reformed" economy, operating on a two-track price system.[11]

When Goh arrived in China in the second half of the 1980s, it was just about the most exciting time for him. China was changing rapidly, reforming and developing all at the same time. China's half-reformed economy was quite messy, presenting all sorts of problems from rent-seeking and corruption to inefficiency and market distortion. Being a practical economist and a former policymaker, it was very much in his element to try to "crack" some of the problems for China. As reflected in his reports for the Chinese government, he acknowledged the enormous difficulties and challenges faced by the Chinese leadership at the time — problems that eventually got out of hand and sparked off the Tiananmen protest. He was thus motivated to learn more about the complicated process of economic and social transformation that was happening in China. In short, Goh's interest in modern China was shaped by both his natural instincts and the special circumstances as an economic adviser to the Chinese government.

When I started work at IEAP, it was still a privately constituted non-profit seeking body, independent from the

---

[11]For more detailed discussion of this subject, see John Wong, "China's Entrepreneurial Approach to Economic Reform", *IEAP Internal Study Paper*, No. 8 (16 February 1995).

National University of Singapore. It was overseen by a management board with Goh Keng Swee as chairman and Ong Teng Cheong (then second deputy prime minister) as vice chairman. Other members included one permanent secretary, the vice chancellor of NUS, the editor of *The Straits Times*, the editor of *Lianhe Zaobao,* as well as two China scholars from overseas, Professor Tu Wei-Ming from Harvard and Professor Wang Gungwu from the University of Hong Kong. The institute's operating revenue came from the Intraco Fund (originally a small tax imposed on Singapore's trading with socialist countries) managed by the Ministry of Trade and Industry (MTI). It was Goh who initiated the Intraco tax and the funding for IEAP was also arranged by him. Subsequently, IEAP got further funding from the Totalisator Board, of which Goh was chairman. It should, however, be noted that Goh had all along been very strict about how this public money was spent, confirming yet again his reputation for frugality.

One day I raised the issue with Goh whether the institute's name should be changed now that its research direction had shifted. Most of the Confucian scholars had already left by then, and none of the new researchers and scholars, including me, was a philosopher. Yet, while we were not Confucian scholars, we still subscribed to the Confucian notion of having a "proper name" for whatever we were doing; the idea of "what is in the name" (名正言顺 or rectification of names) remains important to all the Chinese scholars. However, Goh seemed very "unConfucian" in this regard. His response was relaxed and informal: "Don't rush. Name is not important. More important is whether you all can do good work."

Subsequently, I came to appreciate the underlying political implications. What we were doing at the time was actually researching on "Communist" China, still a politically sensitive subject in Singapore, and more so in the region around Singapore because of Cold War legacies. Singapore established formal diplomatic relations with China only in October 1990, shortly after Indonesia had done so. Back in the early 1980s when Deng Xiaoping had already started economic reform, publications and newspapers from China were still banned in Singapore. Indonesia did not even allow the importation of Chinese books and newspapers regardless of their origins — anything bearing Chinese characters was banned. Even by 1990, news about China seldom appeared on the front page of the local Chinese newspaper *Lianhe Zaobao*.

In the early 1980s, when I subscribed to the *Jingji Yanjiu* (经济研究 or economic research) from Beijing for research purposes, for every issue I had to go down to the Ministry of Culture's "Undesirable Publications Unit" (which also dealt with pornographic publications) to sign an undertaking that this publication was purely for my personal research uses before it was released to me. Later at IEAP, I came to know that even books on Chinese history and philosophy from China, which were ordered by the IEAP library, were also subject to the same censorship. Our librarian had to get clearance from the Controller of Undesirable Publications before the books could be brought into the library. Today, one still find some books at the East Asian Institute (EAI) library with a "Restricted" stamp, meaning that they are not supposed to be used by any unauthorised member of the public.

Because of these Cold War legacies, Goh probably thought it would be better for IEAP to carry on its sensitive research under the cover of classical studies for a start, especially since most of the researchers at that time were from China, with some having complicated political backgrounds. It was only in late 1992, when China had opened up much more after Deng's *Nanxun*, did Goh agree to change IEAP to "IEAPE" or the Institute of East Asian Political Economy. Looking back, this was quite a clever move, as keeping the more or less similar acronym had quietly masked the radical change in the research direction with minimal public fuss.

When I came to IEAP, there were only a handful of former classical scholars left, while a number of new researchers familiar with China's existing political and social situation were recruited directly from the PRC. These were a motley group of former officials associated with the Zhao Ziyang regime — Zhao having been dismissed by Deng for his role in the Tiananmen incident — who were known to Goh or had assisted him in his work in China (including Goh's interpreter). They were all happy to be able to get out of China after the Tiananmen crackdown. Most of them were not dissidents in the sense that they were banned from returning to China. Academically speaking, they were not scholars with training to do research. They were more like interpreters or decipherers of what was going on in China. In any case, Goh found them very useful because they had lived and worked in China, and were therefore capable of providing insider knowledge and first-hand experience on understanding developments in China.

Back in the early 1990s, it was extremely difficult to recruit suitably qualified PRC scholars with training in modern social sciences. I made several trips to the United States, UK and Australia for recruitment purposes, but they were not particularly successful. China in the 1980s had sent quite a number of students abroad for further studies, but only a small proportion of them were in the social sciences, with even fewer seeking to pursue a PhD. In 1991, when I went to the States to do recruitment, I could virtually count with my own fingers the number of PRC students who had obtained a PhD from a good university in Economics, Politics or Sociology. Those who did so would prefer to stay in America, even for a teaching job in a small college. And then not all of them were suitable for our kind of empirical research at the institute: a PhD in Economics, for instance, was likely to be too narrow or too "mathematical" for policy-related studies. In fact, the institute continued to be dogged by this serious recruitment problem through most of the 1990s. Zheng Yongnian came to the institute in 1996. He was the first PRC scholar with a PhD in political science (from Princeton) that the institute had recruited.

A few months after I came to IEAP, a very special researcher arrived at the institute as Senior Research Fellow. Eu Chooi Yip was formerly secretary of the outlawed Malayan Communist Party's Southern Branch, which took charge of Singapore's Communist activities. Eu fled Singapore from the British police, first to Indonesia and later to China, where he lived in exile for many years until Goh arranged for his return to Singapore in 1991. Eu and Goh were classmates and close friends as they both graduated from Raffles College with First Class Honours in Economics.

Eu was widely respected at the institute and we called him "Eu Lao" (elder), not so much because of his close association with Goh, but mainly because Eu was an affable and likeable person. Already in his early 70s when he came back to Singapore, Eu was still very sharp and his English excellent. While Goh's relations with everyone at the institute were mostly quite formal, he was always very relaxed and comfortable with Eu. In fact, when Goh received official Chinese visitors at the institute, he always asked Eu to be present to give him moral support, even though most of the time Eu remained silent.

The institute was later abuzz with activities after Deng Xiaoping in his celebrated *Nanxun* speech singled out Singapore as a country that had achieved both rapid economic growth and good social order — something the Chinese called "spiritual civilisation". He urged China to "learn from Singapore" and later "do better than Singapore". Shortly afterwards, the Chinese Communist Party dispatched a high-level delegation to Singapore, led by Vice Minister Xu Weicheng from its Propaganda Department, for a study trip.[12] Following Xu's visit, about 400 delegations from various PRC localities and organisations visited

---

[12] The delegation returned to China and quickly put out a book, *Xing-jia-bo jing-shen wen-ming* or "Singapore's Spiritual Civilisation" (Beijing: Red Flag Publishers, 1992). The book highlights Singapore's social and cultural development in a very positive manner. It was made available to all Party branches in China, creating a good image of Singapore among the Party grass-roots members throughout China.

Singapore, and many of them came to the institute to hold discussions and exchange views.

Over the years, the institute had participated in many activities connected with high-level official visits from China and Taiwan, including Zhu Rongji's trip to promote the Pudong project and the "Wang-Koo" meeting to discuss the cross-strait (Taiwan) issue. In fact, three of China's politburo members came to the institute to hold discussions with Goh. Many of China's top technocrats today have also been to the institute for various activities, including Zhou Xiaochuan, governor of the People's Bank of China; Ma Kai, minister at the State Council; and Guo Shuqing, president of the China Construction Bank.

Given his practical experience in China and the research support from the institute, Goh became a de facto adviser to the Singapore government on almost all matters related to China. He had regular Wednesday lunch meetings with then Senior Minister Lee Kuan Yew, which provided opportunities for them to discuss developments in China that were already starting to make newspaper headlines.

Goh was a truly complex person. Besides being a politician and a scholar, he would at times want to go into commercial ventures. Once he got a handle on the academic side, he would think of how to capitalise on the academic resources of the institute for commercial purposes. To help Singapore businesses venture into China, the institute established a consultancy arm called the East Asian Consultancy (EAC) to advise companies on setting up operations in China as well as supplying them with relevant data and information.

In retrospect, the institute was essentially performing the functions of a government think tank, with its activities and research findings kept away from the public. Yet the institute was, legally speaking, a private organisation, with Goh Keng Swee and Ong Teng Cheong each holding a nominal one dollar share. At one time, Goh said to me that for the institute to survive in the long term, it would need a good "mother-in-law". So he tried to approach MTI to adopt the institute and put it under its wing through some kind of institutional arrangement. To my surprise, Goh did not succeed in this endeavour.

Later, Goh also mooted the idea of establishing closer institutional links with either NUS or Nanyang Technological University (NTU). He knew that it would be good for the institute as a research organisation to be much more closely associated with the larger academic community given the difficulties faced in recruiting enough academically qualified researchers. The institute as an independent research organisation just could not offer an attractive career structure to potential PhD applicants. At one point, NTU took the initiative of offering a good site for the institute to be re-located there and be associated with it. But Goh did not follow up on this, for reasons unknown to me. Soon after this, Goh's health started to decline and his memory was not as sharp as before. It is difficult to say whether his interest in China had started to wane, but it was obvious to me that he seemed less excited by developments there.

Then, in 1995, Goh came to my office, saying, "I can't continue with the institute forever. I am thinking of asking Wang Gungwu to take over my place as chairman.

I shouldn't think you'll have any problem with him. His international academic standing should help the institute." When Gungwu eventually came over from Hong Kong to become chairman of the institute, Goh went on to become the vice chairman, and he graciously let Gungwu occupy his big office while he took up the small one meant for the secretary next door. He stayed on as vice chairman in order to help ease the leadership transition and, as I understand it, he also wanted to ensure that the institute continued with its existing research focus.

Soon after that, I began a five-month sabbatical and took up the chair of ASEAN Studies at the University of Toronto, a position created by a Canadian government aid agency. Upon my return, I noticed that Goh seldom came to the institute. I thought he might have lost interest in the institute and moved on to something else. Later, when I saw him, he complained that the institute had not produced many new papers and had not been able to hire more new scholars. My temporary absence had not improved the situation.

Before long, Goh called me to his office and said, "The institute has outlived its original usefulness. I told the government that I want to close it down. They may start something new." As it happened, while the legal process was underway to close down IEAPE, another process of creating a new institute was going on simultaneously. Dr Tony Tan, then deputy prime minister and minister for defence, called Wang Gungwu and me to his office to brief us on the setting up of the new institute.

In March 2007, East Asian Institute (EAI) was formally opened by George Yeo, then minister of trade and industry. EAI used the same IEAPE premises, taking over its library, its endowment (S$55 million) and remaining scholars, with Wang Gungwu as director and me as research director. It was constituted as an autonomous university-level research organisation within NUS. Its mission was to conduct both academic as well as policy-related research on China and China's changing relations with its neighbours in East Asia. The institute had thus undergone a double reincarnation: from IEAP to IEAPE and then to EAI. Goh was apparently quite happy with the outcome and he came back to EAI twice.

To fulfil its academic mission, EAI started to organise weekly seminars and regular public lectures. Over the years it has also produced numerous books and journal articles. Wang Gungwu's academic experience and his international academic standing had greatly contributed to this smooth transition from policy-oriented research to both policy and academic research. Meanwhile, its policy-related research has been expanded to meet its public service obligations by regularly circulating informative and policy reports on developments in China and the rest of East Asia to the Singapore government. EAI is probably the only such research institute in Singapore that has successfully main-tained such a good balance between academic and policy-related research. EAI is internationally recognised, particularly in China, as the leading research organisation on modern China in this part of the world.

Adjusting to Policy-oriented Research

When I first started at IEAP in 1990, my immediate problem was not so much to adjust my working relations with Goh as to adapt my own research orientation from publication-based academic research to practical policy-oriented research. Both require sound scholarship as their foundation plus some familiarity with basic methodology and modern social science tools. The difference lies more in the approach as well as the attitude of the researcher. Unlike academic papers, a good piece of policy-related research usually needs to be focused and factual, not meant to test any hypothesis or reach any preconceived conclusion. It also needs to be informative and readable. In the process of my adaptation to such policy-oriented research, I had learnt a great deal from Goh, particularly on how to pick potentially significant research topics and how to package the reports to make them concise and readable. Subsequently, I found the experience and knowledge that I had accumulated very useful to my work when I managed policy-related research at EAI as its research director.

I started off specialising in China's rural and agricultural development for my postgraduate studies in London back in the early 1960s. Before 1979, and regardless of what they did for their PhD thesis, most China economists had to brush up on their knowledge of the rural sector in order to have a good grasp of China's economy, true to Mao's dictum that "agriculture is the foundation of China's economy". From the beginning, Goh urged me to pay more attention to domestic political and economic problems related to Deng's economic reforms, especially industrial reforms in urban areas. Goh said, quite rightly, that once economic reform took hold and industrialisation gathered momentum, the agricultural sector would shrink fast and cease to be the mainstay of the economy.

Goh also did not think much of my previous research on China's economic relations with ASEAN. According to him, if one merely studied a country's external economic relations, it would prove too superficial and not make one a real "country expert". Goh was convinced that one must carefully monitor domestic developments in China in order to understand what is actually happening there. He accorded even lower priority to international relations studies, which in his view was too full of subjective perceptions and opinions. In US-China relations, for example, a China scholar in Beijing would take an entirely different view from an American scholar in Washington, and indeed different American scholars from the left or right would hold different views. It would be hard for our scholars to come up with a very good paper on this subject to 'impress SM (Senior Minister)' Lee Kuan Yew, and indeed many Western scholars and commentators themselves came to Singapore to consult Lee on such issues.

Goh therefore set the main research agenda for IEAP, which was to focus primarily on the domestic political, economic and social development of China, and issues that were directly related to economic reform and development. Such a research agenda still constitutes the mainstay of EAI's research activities today.

Goh frequently dispatched reports and comments on China for me to read, with a slip indicating 'this is worth reading'. On one occasion, he sent me an article from the *Far Eastern Economic Review* about certain developments in China, accompanied by this remark: "The author is not telling us what is happening in China, but only what he wishes to happen there." For many decades, contemporary

China studies in the West, especially in the United States, had come under the influence of the Cold War, focusing largely on problems and negative aspects of developments in China. This so-called "Cold War scholarship" continued well after Deng's economic reform and its legacy is still felt today.

Accordingly, many Western commentaries on China tended to be highly opinionated and heavily biased. Goh wanted us to follow a more "objective" approach to China research, which is as far as possible non-Western and non-PRC in perspective. Looking back, such an approach has served us very well, rendering our research reports more relevant and useful to the Singapore government. In fact, this remains the basic guideline for scholars in EAI today.

Goh noted that America had devoted by far the largest amount of resources to "China watching", both in terms of the number of researchers and amount of data, information and knowledge that had been accumulated. Yet it had spectacularly failed to predict the outbreak of all major events that happened to China, such as the Great Leap Forward (1958–60), the Sino-Soviet split (1959–62), the Cultural Revolution (1966–76), the downfall of the "Gang of Four" (1976) and Deng Xiaoping's return to power (1978).

Knowing that Taiwan had the best "China watching" facilities in Asia, Goh assigned a scholar to go through Taiwan's major research publications on China, including those put out by its military intelligence units (such as *Feiqing yanjiu* 匪情研究 or "bandit studies") through the decades. The conclusion remained the same: no evidence to show that those major events had been accurately predicted or anticipated beforehand. Goh thereby reminded us of the limits of any speculation, scholarly or journalistic, on what would happen in China. He wanted us to adopt this as the cardinal principle: "No foreign China expert knows what is happening inside *Zhongnanhai* (中南海, the residence of China's top leaders)".

The primary mission of IEAP was to update the Singapore government of happenings in China. For this purpose, short, readable research reports were circulated to ministers and permanent secretaries. I wrote the first report as *IEAP China News Analysis* No. 1, which went out on 3 January 1991. This was soon followed by other papers issued under different titles: *IEAP Background Brief, IEAP Commentaries, IEAP Discussion Paper* and *IEAP Internal Study Paper.* In the first two years, most of these papers were written by Eu Chooi Yip and I and Eu also translated into English many papers originally written in Chinese by PRC scholars. Goh himself wrote quite a number of papers and took a great personal interest in them, which had to be approved by him before they were released.

EAI has continued this practice by regularly circulating *EAI Background Briefs* to the Singapore government. I managed this activity as the research director until I retired at the end of 2009, by which time the institute (currently headed by PRC-born contemporary China scholar, Zheng Yongnian) had circulated over 500 *EAI Background Briefs.* Some were responses to particular events, like the rise of Falun Gong, the riots in Tibet or the convening of a Party Congress, while others were based on more in-depth research. Minister Mentor Lee was a regular reader, and he sometimes got back to us for more details or further clarification of certain events. Former minister George Yeo from the start had been interested in our work and he was also very supportive of EAI activities. EAI scholars often went to his ministry to give briefings on current developments in China.

Goh as a China Scholar

Goh was a sound and practical economist in his own right and could be considered a great scholar in terms of what he had written. Was he also a good "China scholar"?

Goh never claimed to be a China scholar in any strict academic sense. We know that he was interested in Chinese philosophy and, later, contemporary China. But he did not publish formal academic writing on China. We never doubted that he had the requisite intellect and training to publish good academic papers on China, if only he could take some time out of his busy schedule to do so. Modern scholarship tends to be highly specialised and technical. As adviser to the Chinese government, Goh had written some good reports (for example, on banking reform) and each of these reports could easily be transformed into a good book on that subject.

Some might call him a good "China watcher", though usage of this term has become more of a derogatory label after the end of the Cold War. A China watcher is today an analyst who just comes up with certain observations about China after going through relevant data and information. Yet Goh was clearly more than that. A China watcher does not have Goh's practical experience as a successful politician, nor his superb intellectual powers. Goh had not only grasped how China's political and economic systems operated, but also developed good insight into many critical issues.

Goh's diverse intellectual background and rich experiences defy simple categorisation, but one can certainly describe him as a first-class "China expert". As mentioned earlier, on account of Deng Xiaoping's gradualist approach to economic reform, China in the 1980s ended up with a messy "half-reformed" economy. Economic growth in that decade tended to fluctuate markedly and World Bank reports identified three so-called "reform cycles" in the 1980s. China's economic policy-makers were constantly frustrated by this recurrent phenomenon: (1) once the government let go or frees up, disorder in market quickly appears; (2) in fear of disorder, government quickly reins in; and (3) once the controls are applied, the whole system comes to a screeching halt (一放就乱 一乱就收， 一收就死 or *yi-fang jiu-luan; yi-luan jiu-shou; yi-shou-jiu-si*). Goh used simple macroeconomic knowledge to explain these recurrent problems to the bewildered PRC visitors. He told them that China not being a fully market-based economy just did not have the built-in automatic "stabilisers" to ease economic fluctuations. China at that time also could not employ any effective monetary and fiscal policies for macroeconomic fine-tuning. This was how Goh applied his practical economic knowledge to the situation in China.

In theory, China is supposed to be a unitary state with all the provinces and localities under the administrative control of one centre in Beijing. In reality, China operates as a kind of a de facto federation, with localities informally enjoying a lot of political and economic autonomy. China scholars have always been baffled by this problem, particularly since the pattern of central-local relationship changes all the time. Scholars often explain such changes in terms of central-local power relations, legal or institutional arrangements and so on. But Goh could put it in simple economic perspective.

In late 1993, he told me to pay attention to China's taxation problem. He made a couple of brief points: "Who pays what taxes? Who collects the taxes?" I did not get his points immediately. As an economist, I would be more interested in analysing the tax burden, the equity issue and its overall public finance impact. I thought such tedious details like paying taxes should rightly belong to a tax accountant or a tax lawyer. At the end of 1993, as I was collecting materials for a paper on taxation, the Chinese government came out with a radical tax reform announcement, spelling out which taxes go to local governments, which to the centre, and which to be allocated for revenue sharing between the centre and localities.

Later, in explaining this landmark reform policy, Goh told us that in time of war, power goes to those who command the military. In peacetime, it is more important to control the economic and financial resources. Thus, Shanghai and Guangdong figure more importantly in Beijing's political calculations because both have delivered a lot of revenue to Beijing. Goh, as former minister for finance, was able to provide a useful economic perspective on the issue of central-local power relations.

By 1996, China's economic reform had made highly impressive progress in most areas — officially, over 95% of the prices were determined by the market. However, the reform efforts fell short in two critical areas: the state-owned enterprise (SOE) reform and the banking reform, with the two actually interrelated. Most China economists, including those at the World Bank, were pondering over how the Chinese leadership could find the best way to tackle this last hurdle of economic reform. They would need strong political will and be prepared to make tough decisions to deal with a whole range of complicated political and social problems. Goh was also thinking hard about how China could best solve this problem.

I distinctly remember Goh's conclusion on the matter: "How can they solve their SOE reform at this stage? Reforming any big enterprise involves restructuring and retrenchment. If you want an SOE to be really subject to the hard budget constraint (i.e. profit maximisation), you have to lay off a lot of workers and even sack the management. The Chinese Communist Party is supposed to be made up of mainly the proletariat. How can they lay off workers at this time without having first established the required social safety network? Even more so for the management, how can they touch those high cadres, their own people?" With that, he shook his head. Goh was absolutely right. Most economists outside China held similar views. The consensus at the time was that reforming SOEs and the banks would be a difficult, long drawn-out process for China.

As mentioned earlier, having to divide his time between IEAPE and other commitments, Goh appeared to have lost interest in China by 1996. If so, the above account goes towards a possible explanation. Since he could not see a quick breakthrough in China's SOE reform, all the rest would just be small, routine developments, which would not be exciting or challenging enough for his highly analytical mind.

Looking back, we had underestimated China's ability and its ingenuity in coping with its own problems. Premier Zhu Rongji did possess the political will to tackle the SOE issue. He also had the patience. First, Zhu started off by modernising the management of the big SOEs. Then, he followed his strategic plans of dealing with different SOEs in a different way, typically by *Zhua-da fang-xiao* (抓大 放小), or concentrating most efforts on the large, strategically important SOEs and letting go or disposing of the smaller ones. Finally, when it came to the critical stage of retrenchment, Zhu used the innovative *xia-gang* (下岗 or off-post) tactic, meaning that the redundant workers were not technically laid off, but merely told to stay at home or look for other jobs while they were still paid a small basic wage, though without bonus or other allowances. It was part of the Chinese way of doing things and had proved effective, particularly compared to the messy "Big Bang" approach adopted in Russia and other former socialist countries in Eastern Europe.[13]

On 3 January 1990, IEAP circulated its first report written by me to the government as *IEAP China News Analysis* No. 1. Goh wrote an interesting foreword for it:

China fascinates and an enormous output of scholarly and journalistic literature has accumulated over the years. But the

---

[13] For further discussion of this subject, see John Wong, "Reforming China's State-Owned Enterprises: Problems and Prospects", *EAI Background Brief*, No. 3 (10 October 1997); and Yang Mu and Tam Chen Hee, "Xiagang: The Chinese way of Reducing Labour Redundancy and Reforming State-Owned Enterprises", *EAI Background Brief*, No. 38 (20 July 1999).

writings often serve to confuse rather than illuminate. Adding to this difficulty in understanding China, Singaporeans in interpreting events in China, like others, unconsciously assume that people there will respond to situations much as we would do in similar situations. Quite often, the Chinese act differently and this adds to our puzzlement.

Goh was acutely aware of the enormous problems faced by foreign China experts in their efforts to interpret events and developments in China. He was also right in reminding Singaporeans that China in those days was under a different system and the people there could behave in a different way.

China today has replaced Japan as the world's second largest economy and is already the world's leading trading nation. China produced most of the world's manufactured products and holds the world's largest foreign exchange reserves. In *Forbes* list of the world's richest people, many are PRC Chinese. Several PRC companies have also made it to the *Fortune's* World Top 20 ranking.

Anybody who travels to China today will find that the Chinese have both capitalist virtues and its vices. In 2009, 50 million Chinese went overseas as tourists. Chinese tourists are now known as "big spenders", as indeed about a third of the world's total luxury goods and designer products are sold in China. Many urban middle-class families have domestic help and of late they also want Filipina maids.[14] How can any Singaporean today say that the PRC Chinese behave differently?

---

[14] See "Many want domestic help from abroad", *China Daily* (17 May 2010).

But Goh made this remark some 20 years ago. No China experts, and in fact no one, including the Chinese themselves, would have predicted China to rise so rapidly. In 2010, more cars were produced and sold in China than in America — over 18 million units. Could anyone have imagined this (Chinese buying more cars than the Americans) 20 years ago? Such are the perils of China watching.

Should China experts run their own self-criticism for having missed the point? Goh would certainly have no problem with this. He had already warned us from the outset that however good we are as outside experts, there are limits to our understanding of China as outsiders, much more so for predicting its future.

Singapore's Road to "China Watching"

John Wong

Professorial Fellow and Academic Adviser,
East Asian Institute, Singapore

Summary

This paper starts with a review of the rise and decline of "China Watching" in the West, which grew out primarily as a product of the Cold War, with a strong political agenda and heavily imbued with ideological biases. But it dominated contemporary China studies during the Cold War period. Following the détente, China watching had also started to adapt. Subsequently, China watching has also evolved and changed as China started its economic reform and open-door policy in the 1980s. The sea change in China watching was actually brought about by the rise of the younger generation of China scholars, including many who were born and bred in China. Better trained in the social science disciplines and having access to field work in China plus the availability of more abundant data, these younger China scholars had virtually put an end to the old-fashioned mode of China watching and "normalised" contemporary China studies.

The development of China watching in Singapore bears some similarities as well as differences from the Western context. It was also heavily influenced by political considerations as it was in fact started under strong government auspices. It went through a rather tortuous process, being shaped by changes in Singapore's domestic politics and its changing relations with China.

China watching in Singapore was initiated by its first deputy prime minister, Dr Goh Keng Swee, who set up the Institute of East Asian

Philosophies (IEAP) in 1983, originally for the purpose of promoting Confucian studies; the research direction was subsequently changed to focus primarily on China watching.

In 1992, IEAP was renamed as the Institute of East Asian Political Economy (IEAPE). Five years thereafter, in 1997, IEAPE was again renamed as the East Asian Institute (EAI) to become an autonomous research organisation within the National University of Singapore. Both IEAP and IEAPE were closed-door think tanks for the Singapore government with their research findings kept out of the public domain. EAI, in contrast, was set up as an open academic organisation charged with the mission of conducting both policy-related and academic research.

From the outset, Singapore has followed its unique approach to China watching, which is as far as possible non-Western and non-PRC. Today, EAI has developed into a foremost research organisation on China in the whole of Southeast Asia. It has continued to circulate its research reports on China and other aspects of East Asia to the Singapore government regularly (ministers and senior civil servants) while encouraging scholars to publish in books and learned journals. EAI has been recently ranked as one of the top five "think tanks" in Asia.

The Old China Hands

"China watching" is an arcane art. Conventionally defined, it refers to modern China studies during the Cold War period by a motley group of "China experts" comprising primarily journalists, analysts from the security or intelligence establishments and academic scholars. Since the term "China watching" was later given a derogatory label, it is not certain if it would be appropriate to call those prominent China scholars such as John K Fairbank, Benjamin Schwarz, Franz Michael, Robert Scalapino, A Doak Barnett, Lucian Pye, Allen Whiting, John Lewis and Michel Oksenberg real "China watchers". Many of their students in those Cold War days could be categorised as such. But the post-Cold War younger generation of China scholars or sinologists would certainly shun this labelling.

The main objective of the China-watching exercise was to explain or to "decipher" what was happening inside Communist China, mainly about short-term events rather than its long-term development. Since Communist China was closed to foreign scholars and foreign journalists, particularly after the collapse of the Great Leap Forward in 1959 when systematic official information and data were no longer available to the public, China watching started to thrive. Western journalists and analysts (including some well-known journalists like Stanley Karnow, Robert Elegant, Robert Keatly, etc.) flocked to Hong Kong to glean information on China by looking for clues from official propaganda, meticulously pouring over reports and events that appeared in the few newspapers and reports that were available outside China, including information from interviewing refugees, defectors and travellers coming out of China and even swapping notes with diplomats and spooks.[1] Their standard techniques include scrutinising top leaders' public appearances (who stood next to whom and whose name was listed above whom) and also the sudden absence of any top leader from public view. By this measure, Mao was rumoured to have died at least 20 times!

In this way, a China watcher was able to piece together bits and pieces of information to build up a picture along with conjectural arguments on what was supposed to be happening in China at a particular point of time. Though it might at times be quite accurate, the outcome was often speculative. But all these do not add up to true contemporary China scholarship, as a typical China watcher does not really "study" China in the same way as a contemporary China scholar would by spending a lot of time and efforts on analysing an issue in depth or testing a hypothesis with more systematic data and observations.[2] While a China watcher often starts off with some preconceived ideas and personal prejudices by concentrating mostly on negative reports or looking mainly at problems (the so-called "problems of communism study") in China, a contemporary China scholar true to the discipline aims to be more neutral and more objective. China watching is therefore at most an imprecise art, which hardly deserves to be called Sinology. China watching is much like "Kremlinology" that was developed to "watch" developments in the Soviet

---

[1] Robert Shaplen, "The China Watchers", *The New Yorker* (12 February 1966).
[2] See Gail Solin, "The Art of China Watching", Centre for the Study of Intelligence <Studies Archive Indexes> Vol. 19, No. 1, Approved for release 1994. CIA Historical Review Programme 2 July 1996.

Union during the Cold War. In short, both China watching and Kremlinology were basically the products of the Cold War.

A New Breed of China Watchers

With the advent of the China-US détente starting with President Nixon's visit to Beijing in 1972, China watching began to slowly lose its credibility and its reputation. Once the Cold War started to thaw, China watching had to struggle to find a useful and relevant role for itself. In the meantime, a group of American graduate students and younger faculty, who opposed the American war in Vietnam, founded the Committee of Concerned Asian Scholars (CCAS) in 1968 and attacked the underlying approach of Asian studies, including China watching, as a form of Cold War scholarship, which was also used by the US government to further its Asian policy of domination and containment of China. Among the CCAS members were some budding and promising second-generation "China watchers" such as Elizabeth Perry, Mark Selden, Edward Friedman, Richard Baum, Orville Schell, Frederick Teiwes and Susan Shirk, who also questioned the fundamental premises of China watching, particularly for its unorthodox ways of information gathering and its inherent ideological biases in their interpretation of events and in drawing their conclusions.[3]

---

[3] Their early views were published in the CCAS journal *Bulletin of Concerned Asian Scholars*. For more detailed discussions, see Richard Baum, "Studies of Chinese Politics in the United States", in Robert Ash, David Shambaugh and Seiichiro Takagi (eds), *China Watching: Perspectives from Europe, Japan and*

Shortly before Nixon's trip to Beijing, Zhou Enlai used "Ping Pong diplomacy" as a means to selectively invite China scholars to visit China, including some young Committee of Concerned Asian Scholars (CCAS) members. It turned out that some of these young and idealistic scholars had swung to the other extreme of easily and uncritically embracing the official views of the Maoist doctrine (e.g. grass-roots democracy and egalitarianism) and certain positive aspects of the Cultural Revolution (the people's communes and the "bare-footed doctors"). Accordingly, they came out of China with glowing reports of what was happening in China based on what they were shown and what they could get from the official rhetoric.[4]

Through the 1970s, China was at the tail-end of the Cultural Revolution, but it was still riddled with political intrigues. The many political ups and downs in this decade include the sudden downfall of Mao's designated heir-in-apparent Lin Biao, the Anti-Confucian Campaign (targeting at Zhou Enlai), the political rehabilitation of Deng Xiaoping, the appointment of Hua Guofeng as Mao's successor and the fall of the Gang of Four. As China was then still off-limits to foreigners with official information still scarce and scanty, China watchers continued to enjoy a great field day throughout the 1970s. In fact, for many years, even after the introduction of economic reform

---

the United States (London, Routledge, 2007). Also, Baum's recent and last work, *China Watcher: Confessions of a Peking Tom* (Seattle and London, University of Washington Press, 2010).

[4] Committee of Concerned Asian Scholars, *China! Inside the People's Republic* (New York, Bantam Books, 1972).

in 1978 with more foreigners touring China and business-men going to China to do business, China was still operating with a modicum of transparency. China watching was not immediately out of business yet!

Entering the 1980s, as post-Mao China had openly discarded its radical revolutionary ideology in favour of market reform and economic development and normalised relations first with the United States and subsequently with the anti-communist ASEAN neighbour, China watching lost its original *raison de'etre* as defined by the Cold War. Its *modus operandi* also had to change as China experts are now increasingly made up of younger scholars, not just better trained in the social sciences but also having greater access to more and better quality data and information. Meanwhile, many veteran journalistic China experts started to retire or just gradually fade away. In their stead were many bona fide China scholars who were not imbued with a strong Cold War mentality.

Most significant of all was the development in which the ranks of the new generation of China scholars, the third generation, were increasingly filled by those who were born and bred in Communist China and who went overseas for post-graduate studies. This group grew up in China during its most turbulent periods and many of them were from families with direct or indirect connection with the local or central leadership. And that started the sea change in the field of China watching. Firstly, one can easily identify sharp ideological differences between the older China watchers and the younger ones. Many old China scholars in the United States, haunted by the McCarthy era of anti-communist fervour, had to show conformity and

loyalty by openly displaying hostility towards any communist regime for fear of being labelled as a communist sym-
pathiser or fellow travellers. Old China scholars everywhere
had to be ideologically hardened to the right in order to be
politically correct, as China watching then was basically a
kind of "enemy study". After the Cold War, young China
scholars eventually did not have to conform to such political and ideological constraints, and they could study China
with a much more open mind, thereby starting the process
of the gradual de-politicisation of contemporary China
studies.

Secondly, whereas old China watchers mostly focused
on political, economic and social development before
1980, particularly on events surrounding Mao's campaigns
such as the Great Leap Forward and the Cultural Revolution,
the new generation of China watchers has focused initially
on China's reform and development after 1980 and subsequently on the rise of China and its regional and global
impact. In terms of methodology, the old hands basically
just chronicled events through laborious historical analyses
and screening of published information while the new
China experts would resort to more sophisticated analytical
tools to examine the increasingly abundant data and comprehensive information made available by the Chinese government (China economists today can actually run
regression and production function on China's economic
and social data). Above all, 'new' China watchers could do
field work and conduct interviews in China.[5] This has

---

[5] See Zhang Zhixin, "Young American China Watchers' View on China",
CIR (January/February 2008). China Institute of Contemporary
International Relations.

made the sea change possible. Accordingly, "China watching" is regaining its proper name as "contemporary China studies".

The Legacies of China Watching

How to evaluate China watching? Since it is not really Sinology in a strictly scholastic sense, it has to be looked at not from the academic angle, but as a policy tool and its contribution to policy making. Without doubt, China watching had served Western media very well during the Cold War days in terms of informing the public about what was going on in China, rightly or wrongly. More importantly, it was primarily used by Western governments to formulate their China policy. At the peak of the Cold War, virtually hundreds of "China analysts" were employed in US intelligence and defence establishments to monitor developments in Communist China.

The next critical question then arises: How effective a tool has China watching actually been? Did it have strong predictive value? If the many China-watching old hands were called back today to make a self-confession, they would readily admit that despite all their efforts and with all the resources available to them in those days, their "trade" did not yield much useful predictive value.

Specifically, the United States had devoted by far the largest amount of resources to 'China watching', both in terms of the number of researchers and amount of data, information and knowledge that had been accumulated. Yet it had spectacularly failed to predict the outbreak of all major events that happened to China during the Cold War, such as the Great Leap Forward (1958–60), the Sino-Soviet split (1959–62), the Cultural Revolution (1966–76), the downfall of the 'Gang of Four' (1976) and Deng Xiaoping's return to power (1978). There are so many known unknowns as well as unknown unknowns in the real world of dynamic power relations, particularly in a closed communist society. China watching simply did not provide the crystal ball to foretell China's future.

Still, China watching has left behind both positive and negative legacies in the field of contemporary China studies to this day. A veteran China-watching old hand had learnt to be very patient and meticulous in gathering basic information, highly cautious in accepting official rhetoric, and extremely careful in assessing and interpreting official publications. Many young scholars in today's internet age have often taken these precautions for granted. Such meticulous and even tedious approach to data collection is still very important for empirical research such as area study today.

On the other hand, as a product of Cold War scholarship, China watching used to be primarily focused on "problems of communism" by highlighting essentially all the negative aspects of development in China. This has left a lasting impact on the Western media today, which still tend to focus and report largely on the negative aspects of China's development and exaggerating China's problems, sometimes even out of context. Thus, many Western commentators still use double standards to judge China's rise, which cannot be "peaceful" and hence the growing "China threat". China's diplomatic initiatives with its neighbours are interpreted as China's "assertive behaviour". When China's economic growth has slowed from 10 to eight per cent (still a highly respectable growth performance by all accounts), it is labelled "hard landing".

True, academic research has to set its focus on problem, and a good scholar must start with scepticism and a good critical mind. However too many China scholars today have inherited the past biases to perpetuate their "problem-oriented" research, artificially and indiscriminately focusing on "alternative explanations" to all official lines. This has resulted in the lack of cool and balanced explanations of developments in China.

Take China's economic rise. China has chalked up near double-digit rates of growth for over three decades to become the world's second largest economy after the United States and it has also lifted record numbers of people out of poverty. From economic development perspective, China's economic and social progress is historically significant in some widely acknowledged positive indicators like poverty alleviation. China scholars have never seriously explained China's economic success. But then China watching from the outset was never meant to provide a balanced conclusion.

China Watching in the Singapore Context

The Decline of Chinese Language Schools

The development of China watching in Singapore bears some similarities but more differences from the Western context. Though China watching in Singapore did not start off as part of the Cold War context as in the West, it was also heavily influenced by political considerations as it was developed under strong government auspices. On the surface, Singapore looks very Chinese, with ethnic Chinese constituting over 70 per cent of its population. In reality, for political reasons, Singapore did not provide a conducive intellectual climate for scholars to become interested in contemporary China studies.

Before its independence, Singapore used to be a "Chinese educational bastion" for Southeast Asia developing a comprehensive Chinese-language education system without government support. Singapore also founded the first Chinese-speaking university outside of China entirely with private efforts, the Nanyang University. However, the Chinese education system had quickly declined after independence as the Singapore government led by Mr Lee Kuan Yew not only did not develop or promote Chinese education, but also suppressed the Chinese newspapers (*Nanyang Siang Pau* and *Sin Chew Jit Poh*) as both were regarded as hotbeds for spreading communism and Chinese chauvinism.[6] Lee recognised how the communist threat could endanger the survival of Singapore in the geo-political context of an anti-communist Southeast Asia. He also realised how Chinese chauvinism could breed communalism, which would threaten the stability of Singapore as a multi-racial society. Thus, the government cracked down on the Chinese newspapers and introduced measures to integrate all schools by starting bilingual education at the primary level, with English as the major

---

[6] For further information, please see Lim Mun Fah, "Chinese education in Singapore: As you sow, so will you reap" *Sin Chew Daily* (26 November 2009); and Thum Pingtjin, "Chinese Language Political Mobilization in Singapore, 1953–63", (PhD thesis for Oxford University, 2011).

medium of instruction leaving Chinese, Malay and Tamil to be taught as mother tongues.

As a result, the Chinese language ability (both reading and writing) of the younger generation of Singaporean Chinese had been weakened. As more and younger Singaporean Chinese started to speak English at home and to each other outside, their Chinese language standard further declined. Since books and newspapers from China were banned in Singapore and visits to China prohibited, young Singaporean Chinese had grown up with very little background knowledge of the history and geography of China. All these had contributed, intentionally and unintentionally, to what may be called the "de-sinification" of the younger generation of Singaporean Chinese. This was regarded as inevitable as the country was intent on developing a stronger Singaporean identity.

Subsequently, the government did encourage the study of more Chinese and to speak more Mandarin by starting the annual "Speak Mandarin Campaign", but it had not effectively reversed this process. This also explains why Singapore had to import China experts from the PRC (People's Republic of China) to carry out its "China watching"!

Not surprisingly, Singapore's road to China watching had gone through a rather tortuous process comprising three phases: (1) the government's sponsorship of classical studies to promote Confucian values by setting up the Institute of East Asian Philosophies (IEAP) in 1983; (2) the reorganisation of the IEAP in 1992 to become the Institute of East Asian Political Economy (IEAPE), a semi-official think tank specifically for China watching; and

(3) the dissolution of the IEAPE in 1997 and the establishment of the more independent East Asian Institute (EAI), an autonomous research organisation within the National University of Singapore. The main mission of EAI, as a member of the wider university community, has gone from the early days of "China watching" to *watching China* and *studying China*.

The key person behind the whole process was the late Dr Goh Keng Swee, Singapore's first deputy prime minister (Mr Lee Kuan Yew's "right-hand man" from the start), having held portfolios in finance, defence and education.[7] Goh was behind Singapore's Confucianism campaign when he was minister of education and chairman of IEAP, which provided the intellectual support to this campaign.

After retiring from politics in 1984, Goh became an economic adviser to the 'Office of Special Economic Zones' of China's State Council under Vice Premier Gu Mu. Goh's China assignment aroused his interest in China's economic reform and development, which in turn made him see the need to start China watching in Singapore.[8]

In 1990, John Wong was appointed by Goh as director of IEAP and later IEAPE. With constant guidance and advice from Goh, Wong's IEAPE started the business of China watching in Singapore. In 1997, IEAPE was renamed EAI, with Wang Gungwu as its director and Wong, the research director. Currently, the PRC-born

---

[7] For Goh's contribution to Singapore's development, including China watching, see Emrys Chew and Chong Guan Kwas (eds), *Goh Keng Swee: A Legacy of Public Service* (Singapore, World Scientific, 2012).
[8] See Zheng Yongnian and John Wong, *Goh Keng Swee on China: Selected Essays* (Singapore, World Scientific, 2013).

Zheng Yongnian has succeeded Wang as director of EAI, after a brief interval of directorship held by Yang Dali in 2007. Zheng first joined IEAPE in 1996, the first PRC scholar with a PhD in political science from Princeton University who was recruited by IEAPE.

Watching China to Understand China at IEAPE

John Wong's immediate mission at IEAP was to change its research focus from classical studies to the study of contemporary China with special emphasis on China's economic reform and political changes, or "China watching" in short. The initial batch of China scholars at IEAP comprised a motley crew of former officials associated with the deposed Zhao Ziyang regime. They were all happy to be out of China after the Tiananmen crackdown. They were not dissidents who were banned from returning to China.

Academically speaking, they were not really scholars who were trained to do research. They were more like interpreters or decipherers of what was going on in China. In any case, they had been very helpful because they had lived and worked in China, and were therefore capable of providing insider knowledge and first-hand experience on understanding developments in China.

In the first two years, "China watching" was carried out under the cloak of Confucian studies, for good political reasons. China watching was actually all about researching on 'Communist' China, which was then still a politically sensitive subject in Singapore, and more so in the region around Singapore because of their anti-communist legacies. Singapore established formal diplomatic relations with

China only in October 1990, shortly after Indonesia had done so. Back in the early 1980s when Deng Xiaoping had already started economic reform, publications and newspapers from China were still banned in Singapore. Indonesia did not even allow the importation of Chinese books and newspapers regardless of their origins—anything bearing Chinese characters, even from Taiwan. In Singapore, even by 1990, news about China seldom appeared on the front page of the local Chinese newspaper *Lianhe Zaobao* while the English newspaper *The Straits Times* used the term "red" for things associated with the PRC.

Partly because of these Cold War legacies, IEAP carried on its sensitive research under the cover of classical studies for a start, especially since most of its researchers at that time were from China, with some having complicated political backgrounds. It was only in late 1992 when China had opened up much more after Deng's *Nanxun* that IEAP proceeded to change its name to "IEAPE" or the Institute of East Asian Political Economy.

The recruitment of suitable researchers posed even greater challenges. Back in the early 1990s, it was extremely difficult to recruit suitably qualified PRC scholars with training in modern social sciences. Wong made several trips to the United States, UK and Australia for recruitment purposes, without much success. China in the 1980s had sent quite a number of students abroad for further studies, but only a small proportion of them were in the social sciences, with even fewer seeking to pursue a PhD.

In 1991, one could virtually count with his/her own fingers the number of PRC students who had obtained a PhD from a good university in Economics, Politics or

Sociology. Those who did so would prefer to stay in America, even for a teaching job in a small college. And then not all of them were suitable for the kind of empirical research at the institute: a PhD in Economics, for instance, was likely to be too narrow or too "mathematical" for policy-related studies. In fact, IEAPE was dogged by this serious recruitment problem throughout.

In the spring of 1992, Deng Xiaoping in his celebrated *Nanxun* speech singled out Singapore as a country that had achieved both rapid economic growth and good social order — something the Chinese called "spiritual civilisation". He urged China to 'learn from Singapore' and later 'do better than Singapore'. Shortly afterwards, the Chinese Communist Party dispatched a high-level delegation to Singapore, led by Vice Minister Xu Weicheng from its Propaganda Department, for a study trip.[9] Following Xu's visit, about 400 delegations from various PRC localities and organisations visited Singapore, and many of them came to IEAPE to hold discussions and exchange views.

Over the years, IEAPE participated in many activities connected with high-level official visits from China and Taiwan, including Zhu Rongji's trip to promote the Pudong project and the "Wang-Koo" meeting to discuss the Cross-strait (vis-à-vis Taiwan) issue. In fact, several members of China's Politburo came to the institute to

---

[9] The delegation returned to China and quickly put out a book, *Xing-jia-bo jing-shen wen-ming* or *Singapore's Spiritual Civilisation* (Beijing: Red Flag Publishers, 1992). The book highlights Singapore's social and cultural development in a very positive manner. It was made available to all Party branches in China, creating a good image of Singapore among the Party grass-roots members throughout China.

hold discussions with Goh. Many of China's top techno-crats today have also been to the institute for various activi-ties, including Zhou Xiaochuan, governor of the People's Bank of China; Ma Kai, minister at the State Council; and Guo Shuqing, chairman of China Securities Regulatory Commission.

China Watching in Action

As IEAP and later IEAPE was charged with the primary mission of conducting policy-oriented research, all new scholars with university teaching experiences and back-ground had to re-adapt their research methodologies and research work from publication-based academic research to practical policy-oriented research. In reality, both require sound scholarship as their foundation in addition to famili-arity with basic methodology and modern social science tools. The major difference lies more in the approaches as well as the attitudes of the researcher. Unlike academic journal papers and monographs, a good piece of policy-related research usually needs to be well-focused and fac-tual, not meant to test any hypothesis or reach any preconceived conclusion. It also needs to be concise, informative and readable.

IEAPE took the view that understanding what was hap-pening in China would require careful monitoring of domestic developments. The institute therefore gave low priority to international relations (IR) studies, a subjective field considered to be heavily influenced by personal per-ceptions and opinions. In discussing US-China relations, for example, a China scholar in Beijing would take an entirely different view from an American scholar in Washington, and indeed different American scholars from the left or right would further hold different views.

Thus, the main research agenda for IEAP/IEAPE was to focus primarily on the domestic political, economic and social development of China, and issues that were directly related to the process of economic reform and development. Such a research agenda still by and large constitutes the bulk of EAI's research activities today. For many decades, contemporary China studies in the West, especially in the United States, had come under the heavy influence of the Cold War environment/rivalries, focusing largely on problems and negative aspects of developments in China. Accordingly, many Western commentaries on China tended to be highly opinionated and heavily biased.

IEAP/IEAPE had made strong efforts to consciously follow a more 'objective' approach to China research, which was as far as possible non-Western and non-PRC in perspective. Looking back, such an objective and neutral approach had served the institute very well, rendering its research reports more relevant and more useful to the Singapore government. In fact, this still constitutes the basic tenet of China watching for scholars at EAI today.

As Taiwan had the best 'China-watching' facilities in Asia, a scholar was assigned to go through Taiwan's major research publications on China, including those put out by its military intelligence units (such as those in the discipline of *Fei-qing yan-jiu* 匪情研究 or 'bandit studies') through the past decades. Even with the facilities and the head-start in modern Chinese studies, their academic output and research conclusions were startling: there is no evidence to show that major events like the Cultural Revolution had been predicted or anticipated beforehand in all the Taiwanese publications before the Revolution. This was a good reminder of the limits of China watching. This has henceforth been the cardinal principle for the institute's China watching: "No foreign China expert knows what is happening inside *Zhongnanhai* (中南海, the residence of China's top leaders)".

The primary mission of IEAP/IEAPE was to update the Singapore government on what was happening in China. For this purpose, short, readable research reports were circulated to Cabinet ministers, ministers of state and permanent secretaries of various ministries. Wong wrote the first report as *IEAP China News Analysis* No. 1, which was circulated to its audience on 3 January 1991. This was soon followed by other papers issued under different titles: *IEAP Background Brief, IEAP Commentaries, IEAP Discussion Paper* and *IEAP Internal Study Paper.*

In the first two years, most of these papers were written by Eu Chooi Yip (former secretary of the outlawed Malayan Communist Party's Southern Branch who just returned to Singapore from his long exile in China) and Wong while Eu also translated into English many papers originally written in Chinese by PRC scholars. In short, IEAP/IEAPE practically functioned as a closed-door government think tank on China, with its research findings kept away from the public domain.

Studying China to Understand China at EAI

In March 1997, IEAPE was closed and renamed East Asian Institute (EAI) to become an autonomous university-level research organisation within the National University of Singapore. EAI's mission is to conduct both academic as well as policy-related research on China (including Taiwan and Hong Kong) and China's changing relations with its neighbours in East Asia. In a sense, this contemporary China studies organisation had undergone a double reincarnation, first from IEAP to IEAPE and then from IEAPE to EAI.

To fulfil its academic mission, EAI started to organise weekly seminars and regular public lectures. Over the past 15 years, EAI has organised many international conferences and workshops on developments in China while EAI scholars have also produced numerous books related to China and other East Asian countries (mainly English but also some Chinese), working papers (both English and Chinese) and journal articles. Besides, EAI publishes two academic journals series, *China: An International Journal*, an internationally refereed journal indexed by Thomson Reuters, and *East Asian Policy*. Looking back, Wang Gungwu's academic experience and his international academic standing had greatly contributed to this smooth transition from policy-oriented research to both policy and academic research.

Meanwhile, its policy-related research has been expanded to meet its public service obligations by regularly circulating (now on a weekly basis) to the Singapore government informative and policy-related reports as *EAI Background Briefs* on the latest developments in China and the rest of East Asia. By the end of 2014, EAI had completed 984 issues of these briefs. Some writings analysed events like the rise and fall of Falun Gong or riots in Xinjiang while many others dealt with developments of topical interest concerning the 18th Party Congress, the National People's Congress and leadership changes at both central and local levels. Still many deal with topics like social protests, housing and health-care reform, pollution and the environment, China's growing relations with the region and with Japan and the United States. These *background briefs* are usually based on more in-depth research and specialisation of the individual scholars. Towards the end of every year, the institute issues *background briefs* reviewing China's domestic political and social development, its economic growth and major changes in its foreign relations in that year. Among the regular readers of the *background briefs* in the Cabinet is Mr Lee Kuan Yew (former prime minister and founding father of independent Singapore).

Besides, EAI often conducts briefings to ministers and senior officials from Singapore's Ministry of Trade and Industry (MTI), Ministry of Foreign Affairs (MFA) and Ministry of National Development on developments in China and Japan. From time to time, the institute was asked by the MFA to brief visiting foreign dignitaries. Over the years, EAI has also been commissioned to undertake consultancy projects for various ministries, including a detailed evaluation of the China-Singapore Suzhou Industrial Park for MTI.

EAI has developed into a foremost research institute on East Asian development, particularly on modern and contemporary China, in the Southeast Asian context. Within Singapore, it is perhaps the only research institute among many others that has maintained a good balance between academic and policy-related research. Recently, an organisation at the University of Pennsylvania has ranked EAI as one of the top five "think tanks" in Asia.

www.ingramcontent.com/pod-product-compliance
Lightning Source LLC
Chambersburg PA
CBHW070923150426
42812CB00049B/1399